AVON FREE PUBLIC LIBRARY
281 COUNTRY CLUB ROAD, AVON CT 06001

THROUGH THE HABITRAILS

Life Before and After My Career in the Cubicles

JEFF NICHOLSON

Foreword by **Matt Fraction**

Introduction by **Stephen R. Bissette**

AVON FREE PUBLIC LIBRARY
281 COUNTRY CLUB ROAD, AVON CT 06001

GRAPHIC
NIC
c.1

DOVER PUBLICATIONS, INC.
Mineola, New York

Copyright

Copyright © 1994, 1996, 2016 by Jeff Nicholson
Foreword copyright © 2016 by Matt Fraction
Introduction copyright © 1996 by Stephen Russell Bissette
All rights reserved.

Bibliographical Note

Through the Habitrails: Life Before and After My Career in the Cubicles, first published by
Dover Publications, Inc., in 2016, is a reprint of the work originally published as *Through
the Habitrails by Bad Habit,* Petaluma, California, in 1996. The story "Cat Lover" is not
included in this edition. A new Foreword and an Epilogue have been provided specially for
the Dover edition.

Library of Congress Cataloging-in-Publication Data

Nicholson, Jeff.
    Through the habitrails : life before and after my career in the cubicles / Jeff Nicholson ;
introduction by Stephen R. Bissette ; foreword by Matt Fraction.
        pages cm. — (Dover graphic novels)
    ISBN-13: 978-0-486-80286-2 (paperback)
    ISBN-10: 0-486-80286-8 (paperback)
    1. White collar workers—Comic books, strips, etc. 2. Graphic novels. I. Title.
PN6727.N49T48 2016
741.5'973—dc23
                                                                    2015029887

Manufactured in the United States by RR Donnelley
80286801   2016
www.doverpublications.com

FOREWORD

Matt Fraction

What, you think YOUR job sucks?

The guy in *Through the Habitrails* has a job that involves getting taps installed in the back of his neck so his ghoulish bosses can drain him of his juice. His main boss is apparently a gigantic, fat little bastard of a gerbil wearing a crown. The job gets so bad that he fashions a jar around his head so he can remain pickled in beer all the time. He has to live with his coworkers, professional politics intermingling inescapably with the personal. These coworkers are egomaniacs, sycophants, drug burnouts, or hollow shells of humans living in cages. He dates some of them, anyway.

The thing is, I know how he feels.

Through the Habitrails is creepy. Genuinely, sincerely creepy. Writer-artist Jeff Nicholson has crafted it with an air of manic desperation and unrelenting horror so vibrant and hallucinatory that it had to, had to, had to really happen. Sure, Nicholson wasn't literally employed by a bastard gerbil, and there were neither neck-taps nor headjars of beer. Yet the feeling Nicholson infuses in this dark, droning faux-memoir is so true, so real that I can't pick up *Habitrails* without flashing back to MY worst-job-ever and recoiling at the cold, sick and familiar feeling it instills in my belly all over again. I can't imagine Nicholson being particularly enthused about *Habitrails* anymore— and this is pure conjecture on my part— as it reads like the frantic, hysterical journal of a man at the end of his rope, replete with all the self-pity and misery usually contained therein.

Neck-taps, dude. Neck-taps.

NEVER ON MONDAY:
THROUGH THE 21ST CENTURY HABITRAILS

Stephen R. Bissette

"If you go into it without being able to find humor, you will see only despair."

—Jeff Nicholson, describing Through the Habitrails to me (1990)[1]

"What a fate: to be condemned to work for a firm where the slightest negligence at once gave rise to the gravest suspicion! Were all the employees nothing but a bunch of scoundrels, was there not among them one single loyal devoted man who, had he wasted only an hour or so of the firm's time in the morning, was so tormented by conscience as to be driven out of his mind and actually incapable of leaving his bed?"

—Franz Kafka, *Die Verwandlung / The Metamorphosis* (1915)

***

This is the only graphic novel I can think of that I would open with the following caveat, "a warning to the curious," as M. R. James might say:

Don't read any part of Through the Habitrails on a Monday.

Tuesday, maybe.
Wednesday to Friday, OK.
Saturday is good, possibly ideal, but only if you don't let the reading spill into Sunday, and by no means wait until Sunday night to either dive in or wrap it up.
But never, ever read this on Monday.

It's been a quarter-century since I first laid eyes upon the initial panels and pages of *Through the Habitrails*, and in all those years, Jeff Nicholson's *Habitrails* has only become a more painfully urgent and relevant metaphoric universe.

I wish it were otherwise—and I'm pretty sure I can speak for Jeff Nicholson when I write that he wishes it were otherwise—but damned if it isn't so. Since North America plunged into its second major economic Depression in 2008, unionization and labor interests have only become more politically demonized and marginalized, and work-places and employment abuses in all walks of life have only become more normalized and deplorable. This situation fully extends into the creative marketplace and free-lancing in industries producing and/or mining intellectual properties. Given my own advocacy for creator's rights in the comics and graphic novels field over the decades, I

---

[1] Jeff Nicholson, quoted in the text introduction to the debut publication of the *Through the Habitrails* "Jar Head" chapter in Taboo 5 (1991, SpiderBaby Grafix & Publications/Tundra Publishing, Ltd.), pg. 19.

am constantly asked to look at various contracts and documents relevant to freelance creative work. I can only tell you this: in many ways, the field has only become more ruthless since the year 2000, the conditions of employment more odious, the contracts more all-encompassing and voracious in their insistence upon total and absolute corporate ownership of any and all creative thought, fruits, and/or labor.

The second installment of *Through the Habitrails* was the one-pager "It's Not Your Juice."

In corporate America, quite the contrary is true.

In fact, many corporations now insist upon total and absolute ownership of intellectual properties *prior to contracting:* thus, demanding unquestioning servitude as a condition of *possible* employment. Consider how most so-called "submission agreements"—contracts that *must* be signed before an art director or appointed representative will even look at a new freelancer's portfolio or creative work, in which freelancers have (as my legal counsel once put it) "zero negotiating power"[2]—insist upon creators acknowledging up front that it's *already* "their juice."

Don't take my word for it. "Submission forms" pre-emptively claiming any and all rights to whatever you have in your portfolio *before you've even shown it* are now a standard practice among many entertainment and publishing corporate firms. As TV animation writer, producer, director, and animator Mark Mayerson wrote in November 2012, many potential employers assume, presume, and assert "*...ownership of your portfolio material when you apply for the job. If you are submitting samples of work you have done for other companies, [the potential employer] wants you to assign the rights to them. You clearly don't have the authority to do that for work you don't own, so that means that you are not legally allowed to show [the potential employer] work you've done for other companies. Sort of defeats the purpose of a submission portfolio, doesn't it? What's clearly disturbing, though, is that any original work in your portfolio becomes their property. This does not depend on whether they hire you or not, they get ownership because you applied.*"[3]

You see, Jeff Nicholson had it dead right.

It's not their juice.

But more and more, corporate America insists *it is.*

The invisible hand of the employer is driving the tap into throbbing "talent" temples before "talent" has even scored the job.

It's a simple verbal surgical procedure to remove four letters from the title of Jeff's second chapter to make it read "It's Our Juice," a corporate credo enforced by a plethora of legal constructs claiming as its own all manner of properties, manufactured, intellectual, and even emotional.

Always read the fine print . . . especially on Mondays.

※

Through the Habitrails originally saw print in 1991—before now-revered pop companions like Mike Judge's feature film *Office Space* (1999) or the TV series The Office (UK original debuted July 2001; U.S. series March 2005) even existed.

While white-collar business satire in all media was a venerable tradition—from, say, Pre-Code Hollywood movies like Michael Curtiz's *Female* (1933) to Shepherd Mead's 1952 satiric novel *How to Succeed in Business Without Really Trying: The Dastard's Guide to Fame and Fortune* (1952) and the Pulitzer Prize and Tony Award-winning musical

---

[2]See Bissette, "Pop Injustices of 2012: A Roundup of Some of the Worst of the Year," *Myrant*, December 28th, 2012, archived at http://srbissette.com/?p=16319

[3]Mark Mayerson, "More Artist Exploitation," Mayerson on Animation: Reflections on the Art and Business of Animation, Tuesday, November 20, 2012, archived at http://mayersononanimation. blogspot.ca/2012/11/more-artist-exploitation.html

(1961) and movie (1967) spun from it—I hasten to point out as a genre white-collar corporate parody was a relative rarity in comics. Mainstream comic book editors and creators kidded themselves in series or stories lampooning the editorial offices of comic book publishers, as in Sheldon Mayer's "Scribbly"—Mayer's semi-autobiographical strip about a struggling young cartoonist initially created for Dell Comics' *The Funnies and Popular Comics* from 1936–39—or the occasional ACG (American Comics Group) and EC Comics Pre-Code horror and science-fiction stories set in the ACG or EC Comics offices, or instances in which Stan Lee used the Marvel bullpen creators and staff as characters (as in *Not Brand Echh!*, 1967–69). The tradition even spilled into the underground comix, as in Tom Veitch and Greg Irons' lead story in *Slow Death* #5 (1973, Last Gasp), in which they rescue their publisher, Ron Turner, from alien possession by the parasitic Shuggahoo.

In those cases, the comic books were inviting the readers to laugh at their glib caricatures of what went on "behind the scenes," never revealing how the business actually worked. One attempt to dig deeper in an unpublished *Secret Origins* installment of Robert Loren Fleming and Keith Giffen's satiric *Ambush Bug* (circa 1990, DC Comics)—a story satirizing the sad plight of DC Comics editors—got its editor promptly and unceremoniously fired. Jack Kirby's savaging of his former Marvel creative partner and editor Stan Lee as "Funky Flashman" in the pages of Kirby's Mister Miracle (#6, January–February 1972, DC Comics) was the rare exception, mocking both Lee and Roy Thomas ("Houseroy"). Kirby's parody only saw print because its publisher, DC Comics, was in direct competition with Marvel Comics, where Stan Lee and Roy Thomas worked at the time. Self-scrutiny, much less insightful public self-analysis, was *never* a characteristic of comic book publishing.

Through the Habitrails debuted only two years after Scott Adams's *Dilbert* strip had surfaced (via United Media Syndicate on April 16, 1989), and before the first book collection of Dilbert strips (which was *Dilbert: Always Postpone Meetings with Time-Wasting Morons*, October 1992). The two are light years apart in intent, content, and impact, however; where *Dilbert* enjoys celebrity based in part on its double-edged satiric sword that serves corporate employers' needs as readily as it feeds white-collar workers' frustrations with management, Nicholson's *Habitrails* absolutely seethes with anger and primal dread of the office space and its toxic effects on the individual and collective workers. In his book about the cultural impact of Adams's *Dilbert* strip, *Media Beat* columnist Norman Solomon once cited how internal Xerox corporate use of certain *Dilbert* strips revealed the complicity tucked within popular "office" comedies like *Dilbert*, despite appearances: "*. . . Xerox management had recognized what more gullible* Dilbert *readers did not:* Dilbert *is an offbeat sugary substance that helps the corporate medicine go down.*" If corporate media did not sanction Dilbert's caustic witticisms, corporate newspapers would not publish Dilbert, nor would Xerox have put various Dilbert strips to their own use. "*The* Dilbert *phenomenon accepts—and perversely eggs on—many negative aspects of corporate existence as unchangeable facets of human nature. . . . As Xerox managers grasped,* Dilbert *speaks to some very real work experiences while simultaneously eroding inclinations to fight for better working conditions.*"[4] Dilbert creator Scott Adams shrugged off the attack from Solomon, but the longevity of the strip and the genre inherently demonstrates its use to corporate media concerns.

If such satire was truly effective, it would arguably cease to exist, or at least be harder to find. If it were truly effective, corporate media venues would deny it distribution.

---

[4] Norman Solomon, *The Trouble With Dilbert: How Corporate Culture Gets the Last Laugh* (1997, Common Courage Press), with its original website and presence archived at http://web.archive.org/web/20040218235653/http://free.freespeech.org/normansolomon/dilbert/book/

One must ask, then, is this a primary function of white-collar satire in *all* corporate media, regardless of the creators' intentions? Does that function skew away from easy corporate reapplication when the comedy becomes too pitch-black, too savage? What if the creative expression moves into another genre: horror? Is it more genuinely effective when it does not emerge from corporate venues (i.e., syndicates), or does broader distribution via corporate media venues ipso facto corrupt, co-opt, undermine, and convert any originally-intended creator intent?

This line of thought inevitably prompts inherently absurdist questions: Was *Through the Habitrails* vital and razor-sharp when it was originally independently published in *Taboo*, then self-published by its creator? Has time and the fact it's now in print via Dover Books changed its chemistry, its intent, its content, its impact? It's the same work (slightly edited and revised, yes), from the same creator. How can its publication venue (*Taboo*, self-publishing, and now Dover Books) in any way alter its intent, content, value, and impact?

If anything, the ongoing popularity of *Dilbert*, *Office Space*, and *The Office* make *Through the Habitrails* more unapologetically accessible, its pitch-black humor something a wider readership is more attuned to.

In many ways, Nicholson's *Through the Habitrails* was contemporary to the distinctive strain of late 1980s–1990s genre fare characterized by film scholar Barry Keith Grant as "yuppie horror," including novels like Bret Easton Ellis's *American Psycho* (1991) and Michael Crichton's *Disclosure* (1994, filmed the same year) and films such as *After Hours* (1985), *Fatal Attraction* (1987), *Pacific Heights* (1990), *Bad Influence* (1991), *Single White Female* (1992), *The Temp* (1993), among others. While this cycle cohered as such when it did, it, too, had roots in older archetypes, including works like Rod Serling's teleplay *Patterns* (January 12, 1955, adapted to film 1956). Grant argued that the 1980s–1990s works "form a distinct generic cycle that, instead of expressing the repression and contradictions of bourgeois society generally . . . specifically address the anxieties of an affluent culture in an era of prolonged recession."[5]

It's highly unlikely that Jeff Nicholson's Gerbil King might rub elbows with the malicious managers tormenting their employees in *The Player* (1992) or *Swimming with Sharks* (1994); if anything, *Through the Habitrails* countered this cycle by focusing on the *employees* subject to the whims of sociopaths like Bret Easton Ellis's Bateman, or the types cited by Grant in his essay on "yuppie horror": "DINKS (Double Income No Kids), WOOFS (Well Off Older Folks), and SWELLS (Single Women Earning Lots and Lots) . . . [or] the indelicate and cumbersome UHBs, or Urban Haute Bourgeoisie…"[6] I'll leave it to you to work up your own acronym for GERBIL.

Through the Habitrails, like *Office Space*, instead shifted its focus to those trapped (by employment) beneath the thumb of the young urban professionals ("yuppies"). These young urban professionals were thriving in upper management positions; their absolute embrace of emerging technologies, ruthless capitalism, and conspicuous consumption made employee conditions increasingly uncomfortable as the shift in wealth increasingly consolidated upwards and wages for the working class in blue-collar and white-collar jobs stagnated. Nicholson's unnamed protagonist would have been the nominal *threat* had he made an appearance in one of the "yuppie horror" entries.

If anything, *Through the Habitrails* might be tentatively associated with such comparatively clumsy fusions of white-collar horror, black comedy, and cubical melodrama

---

[5]See Barry Keith Grant's essay on "yuppie horror" in *Journal of Film and Video* ("Rich and Strange: The Yuppie Horror Film," vol. 48, Spring/Summer 1996), revised for *Planks of Reason: Essays on the Horror Film, Revised Edition* (2004, Scarecrow Press), pp. 153.
[6]Grant, *Ibid.*, pg. 154.

as Cindy Sherman's psycho-killer horror movie *Office Killer* (1997, the very same year Nicholson's unofficial and unacknowledged "sequel" to *Habitrails*, "Day's Work, Night's Rest," was published as *The Dreaming* #15, August 1997, DC Comics/Vertigo; more on that later). But that association does a great disservice to Nicholson's masterwork. Sherman, of course, was and is a celebrated darling of urban photography and high-art circles, but *Office Killer* can't hold a candle to *Through the Habitrails*. I could easily mount an argument for Jeff Nicholson being as striking a visual artist and stylist as Cindy Sherman, but Sherman doesn't come close in either her sole feature film or her photographic gallery pseudo-narratives to Nicholson's conceptual ingenuity or storytelling skills. The fact that there is an entire book dedicated to Sherman's lone feature film, *Cindy Sherman's Office Killer: Another Kind of Monster* by Dahlia Schweitzer (2014, Intellect Ltd/The Mill/University Press of Chicago Press), gives me hope that Nicholson's masterpiece will one day enjoy similar (and more richly deserved) academic analysis in short order.

Surely, the associations and echoes between Nicholson's *Through the Habitrails* and Franz Kafka's nightmarish novels and short stories invite such scrutiny. From the first moment I laid eyes on the one-page story "It's Not Your Juice," the initial incarnation of *Through the Habitrails*, I recognized the kinship. Nicholson's unnamed protagonist and Kafka's K. and Gregor Samsa were soul mates separated only by oceans and time. As Gregor stated in Kafka's *The Metamorphosis*, "He was a tool of the boss, without brains or backbone . . ."

I don't mean to make too strong an associative link with Kafka. We live in an age when the term "Kafkaesque" has become as overused and abused as "Mickey Mouse," "for sure," "awesome," and the omnipresent "whatever." I find it curious that most people eager to slap the term onto any aspect of their existence they find needlessly oppressive (i.e., phone companies, the government, the IRS, home-shopping network, etc.) will admit, upon questioning, that they've never read a line of Franz Kafka. (If you haven't read any of Kafka's works, or don't even know who Kafka is, remedy the situation immediately. Ready now? Good. Let's continue as if you always knew what I was talking about).

Kafka's name has taken on a household mystique, as if it were a trademark associated with a very specific and instantly recognizable product. Thus, at a time when Kafka's few surviving works are relevant to our own times, his name has almost ceased to mean anything. It's as if Kafka had become a scary sibling of Walt Disney and Betty Crocker. In the wake of Victor Hugo's Quasimodo joining the ranks of Dumbo, Pinocchio, and Bambi, perhaps the Disney animated musical version of *The Metamorphosis* isn't too far away (complete with "Gregor and the Apple" play sets and the inevitable McDonald's Happy Meals merchandising). Would Kafka's Castle seem out of place in the Magic Kingdom, or would it eloquently externalize the grim realities of a culture in the thrall of one of the world's most powerful corporations? (I've heard some pretty horrific accounts of working for the Mouse from friends who've worked for Disney's creative divisions, and for Disney World.[7])

---

[7] Don't take my word for it. See John Marr's fanzine *Murder Can Be Fun* article "Death At Disneyland: Waiting in Line to Die," originally published in *Murder Can Be Fun* #13 (1991), revised and expanded for *Murder Can Be Fun* #20 (2007), archived online at https://jplzinelibrary.wordpress.com/2010/08/18/murder-can-be-fun-vol-13/ . I also recommend David Koenig's books on the subject *(Mouse Tales: A Behind-the-Ears Look at Disneyland, The People v. Disneyland: How Lawsuits & Lawyers Transformed the Magic, Realityland: True-Life Adventures at Walt Disney World, Mouse Under Glass: Secrets of Disney Animation & Theme Parks, More Mouse Tales: A Closer Peek Backstage)* and (with caveats: the first two books aren't very well written) *Death in the Tragic Kingdom: An Unauthorized Walking Tour Through the Haunted and Fatal History of Disney Parks* by Keaton Moll (2014, Theme Park Press), *Disney Declassified: Tales of Real Life Disney Scandals, Sex, Accidents and Deaths* by Aaron H. Goldberg (2014, Quaker Scribe), and Leonard Kinsey's *The Dark Side of Disney* (2011, Bamboo Forest Publishing)

Through the Habitrails was and is set in an eerily familiar workplace, where the employees (including Jeff's nameless protagonist, our nominal "hero") labor over an apparently unending flow of production and design work.

They are all periodically tapped, like maple trees, of their creative juices—working "saps," being sapped—a condition of employment they resent but resign themselves to.

We find out precious little about these "jobs" or the corporate proprietors: like the workers, we become painfully acclimated to the corporate offices themselves, networked—and perhaps even serving—the gerbils who scamper and skeedaddle through a maze-like labyrinth of Habitrail tubes and passageways, their purposes unfathomable but unquestioned. We know even less about these gerbils or (shudder) the Gerbil King.

I once summed up Jeff's masterwork as "original, completely absorbing, and deeply, deeply disturbing," and I still count it as one of the best graphic novels of our generation. Jeff's vivid absurdist portrait of a creative spirit trapped in the soul-crushing banality of a corporate workplace is harrowing, alien, and yet utterly familiar. The landscape is unmistakable: the drudgery of the workplace infested with endless gerbil Habitrails; the insidious, unseen superiors physically tapping workers for their sap; depleted and depleting coworkers unable to connect with each other, wallowing in their own personal hells, features obscured, even swallowed, by their addictions.

Jeff's protagonist sports an ultimate "pokerface": a mask, a callous, a shield with the opacity of a reptile's visage.

I often compare the act of storytelling to that process of playing cards, specifically certain poker strategies. When do you show which card? Why? What card do you keep close to your vest? *Through the Habitrails* amply demonstrates the comparative value of the metaphor—and Nicholson was never a shrewder (or crueller) card-player/storyteller. Chapters like "Escape #1: 'El Muerte'," "Escape #2: The Dry Creek Bed,"[8] and "Escape #3: Concow" only tighten the emotional thumbscrews. Nicholson depicts time away from the workplace and the all-important T.G.I.F. weekends—time spent in fleeting recuperative reflection, and hoped-for "healing"—as being fraught with peril and as potentially traumatizing as the daily work week's office space. The contemplation of alternatives to their lives only antagonizes his characters, deepening their employment-imposed woes and self-inflicted wounds.

——◦◉◦——

This first-ever mass-market edition of *Through the Habitrails* reaches your hands in an era in which memoir graphic novels are very much in vogue. This remains a Kafkaesque semi-memoir, a snapshot of an aspect of the creator's working life in the late 1980s and early 1990s—of the day job that fed him, even as it drained him, reinterpreted and filtered through his self-motivated hours at the drawing board at home, after hours.

Some may argue against my classification of *Habitrails* as horror, per se. I consider *Habitrails* a key work of a genre I refer to as "working-class horror," but there is another genre association at work here. As both editor and reader, I first experienced *Habitrails* during the first wave of American memoir comics. *Through the Habitrails* was created and first published when Cleveland's own Harvey Pekar, with his *American Splendor*, was still spearheading that quiet revolution, as had quieter-still Sam Glanzman with his "U.S.S. Stevens" stories for DC Comics (predating the launch of *American Splendor*) and his two-volume graphic novel *A Sailor's Story* (now back in print via Dover, and highly recommended). Both Glanzman and Pekar were naturalistic in their dramaturgy,

---

[8]Note that this chapter of *Through the Habitrails* was nominated for an Eisner Award ("Best Short Story") in 1992.

avoiding sensationalism, fantasy, metaphor, or anything that might detract from or devalue the life-as-it-is-lived realism of their non-fiction comics. But fantasy and metaphoric imagery per se isn't necessarily antithetical to memoir comics: consider, for instance, how central religious iconography, fanaticism, wet-dream visions and feverish delusions are to one of the early essential memoir graphic novels, Justin Green's *Binky Brown Meets the Holy Virgin Mary* (1972, Last Gasp).

Nicholson has been a bit contradictory and evasive about the autobiographical nature or quotient of *Through the Habitrails* over the years. He was quite direct in his disavowal in the Foreword to the first collected edition of *Habitrails* (dated January 22, 1994), writing, ". . . Through the Habitrails *is in itself a recollection, a process, a peril, and an editorial on life. I can't add to that on this page. I just want to add a basic disclaimer to the potential obtrusive reviewer."* Nicholson explained, *"I dread the thought of anyone thinking* Habitrails *is a near-literal representation of my life. I would not want to meet the central character in* Habitrails, *and would prefer not to be confused with him. That distinction would seem obvious, due to the heavy surrealism you are about to witness, but I have already had people assume too much of my private life through this work. Some degree of autobiography is evident, but it is only inner mumblings being reconstructed as a world of its own, with its own symbols, analogies and behaviors. It is a dark world, with violence, depravity and self-destruction. I do this to confront the reader with his or her own inner mumblings in an entertaining way, not to make my own 'cartoon confessional.' Sorry to have bored those of you who would not have made this journalistic assumption. . . ."*

And yet, Nicholson invited the confusion and conflation. On the back cover of both self-published editions of the collected graphic novel, Nicholson himself referred to the readers putting themselves *"in the place of Nicholson's semi-autobiographical nameless hero,"* and he included a portrait of what appeared to be his protagonist above his personal biography in the first edition of the collected *Habitrails*. That biography was telling, too, citing Nicholson's having *". . . worked as an illustrator/ad designer for the* Chico News & Review *from 1988–1990. He began* Through The Habitrails *in late 1989 and finished in late 1992. . . ."* Draw your own conclusions. A few lines later, Nicholson noted (citing himself in the third person), *"He returned to full-time employment outside comics in June of 1993, mid-way through the production of* Lost Laughter #2. *He forsake [sic] the commercial illustration/ad design career of his past and returned to landscape maintenance and is quite content there."* There's been a lot of water under the bridge since then.

I also have the recollection of my phone calls with Nicholson during the years in which *Through the Habitrails* was initially created and published. While I can intellectually separate Jeff Nicholson from his creation, I cannot emotionally detach from the experience of working with Jeff and of how he talked about *Habitrails* in the early 1990s. As he stated in his 1994 Foreword, there was synthesis and symbiosis at work, at play, and however much I recognize Chad Woody's personality in the lettering, that's all Nicholson coming through loud and clear in the voices and visions, the writing and drawing.

We cannot help it as creators: we are what we write, we are what we draw, however emphatically we may insist upon the distance between ourselves and our self-expressions.

Jeff's contribution to the memoir comics revolution was in its way essentially autobiographical, reflective of his own experiences in the American workplace; but it was, and remains, *outside* of that tradition, too. *Through the Habitrails* is autobiographical in the ways that Franz Kafka's *Metamorphosis* and *Das Schloss / The Castle* (1926) and David Cronenberg's *The Brood* (1979) were autobiographical: Jeff uses the lens of fantasy to offer a sharper cartography of reality, the banal but harsh realities business-as-usual overtly refutes even as it covertly depends upon an ever-changing diversity of suffocating, insatiable working environments (including, in the 21st century, the home office: truly, there is no rest for the employed).

What makes *Through the Habitrails* more vital, though, is its harrowing introspection of the transformative process of labor and laboring within such demanding workplaces. Anticipating the coming reality of how digital-device conflation of home, personal life, professional life, and labor would reconfigure all aspects of 21st-century laborer pathologies and biology, Nicholson arrived at jarring images such as that on page 5 of the chapter "Be Creative," revealing his protagonist's self-surgical solution to wanting "all my booze and all my food and all my sex and all my hobbies all my TV all my projects my paintings my band my escape journeys all now . . . RIGHT NOW." There are many similar prescient concepts in late-20th-century comics history—Jack Kirby's "Motherbox" concept in his so-called Fourth World series of the early 1970s *(Jimmy Olsen, The New Gods, Forever People, and Mister Miracle)*, for instance—but few as terrifyingly singular as Nicholson's. I used to keep a photocopy of that page on my studio corkboard: that's how strongly it resonated for me. That image of Nicholson's protagonist pretty much sums up our "plugged in" culture today, though the manufacturers of the devices and apps keeping us forever plugged in have skillfully avoided such Cronenbergian self-mutilation to facilitate similarly transformative "plugging in."

Tell me this isn't horrific—and agonizingly "true."

It was *Cerebus* creator and self-publishing comics pioneer Dave Sim who introduced me to Nicholson's *Habitrails*. At the time, I was editing and co-publishing an ambitious adult horror comic anthology entitled *Taboo* (eight volumes, 1988–1992, with two posthumous volumes subsequently published in 1995). As the original financier and "godfather" of *Taboo*, Dave mailed me photocopies of the first two installments, suggesting (in Dave's rather offhand way) they might, maybe, find a suitable home in the pages of *Taboo* (I always listened to Dave, because the son of a gun is always right, but I was usually too dim to respond properly to Dave's recommendations. Thankfully, I was actually, really listening to him, just this once).[9]

Like many cartoonists, Nicholson had hand-drawn his own comic books (each one-of-a-kind) in grade school and junior high school, culminating in "fully inked, colored, and hand-bound mock-up 32 page comics" that included "6 issues of *Ultra Klutz* (a torturous parody of *Ultraman*), 4 issues of *The Justice Chumps* (a superhero parody), 4 issues of *Alpha Centauri* (a sci-fi series), and 3 issues of *Shnerd* (a parody anthology) . . ."[10] Jeff once told me he'd created *Ultra Klutz* "as a classroom distraction" when he was eleven years old, growing up in the San Francisco Bay area. These hand-crafted one-of-a-kind issues were only seen by friends, family, and classmates; he also began playing music in his teenage years, but "unlike comics, which I later made a career of, playing and recording music always remained a hobby for me."[11] Nicholson's career in comics proper began with the self-publication of *Ultra Klutz* #1 (1981), which I'll get into momentarily.

In the real world, he earned his BA in Communications from California State University in Chico, California, and "worked in the field of landscape maintenance through college" (according to Jeff's short biography in the 1994 Bad Habit collected edition of *Habitrails*). Throughout this period, Nicholson's comics creations surfaced in a variety of fan publications: Jeff's strip "Superhero Overdose" appeared in the weekly tabloid fandom staple *The Comic Buyer's Guide* (1984–86), and he also contributed strips and one-shot stories to various issues of *Fandom Times* (1984–85), *Fandom Teamup*

---

[9]For the sake of history, I must note that Dave Sim included the first-ever public preview of *Through the Habitrails in Cerebus* #133 (Aardvark-Vanaheim, April 1990).

[10]Jeff Nicholson, "Proto-Comics: 1975-1979," archived at http://fatherandsontoon.com/jeffchron. html

[11]Nicholson, Ibid., "Music: 1980-1992."

(working with Tim Corrigan, 1985), *Allies* (with John Howard, 1985), and the reprint series *Giant-Size Mini-Comics* (issues #2 and 4, Eclipse Comics, 1986–87). Nicholson launched into a controversial attack on small press delusions in his self-critical screed *Jeff Nicholson's Small Press Tirade* (1989); a subsequent self-published trade paperback reprint of the latter also included reprints of many of Nicholson's fan comics creations *(Nicholson's Small Press Tirade and Other Works: 1983–1989*, 1994, Bad Habit).[12] Jeff was also a filmmaker throughout these years, experimenting with animation and live-action shorts (1978–1987; he collected his short films on the long out-of-print self-distributed videocassette compilation *Onward Video* in 1990).

It was Jeff's work as the self-publisher of *Ultra Klutz* (1981–92) I was most familiar with. *Ultra Klutz* was an offbeat, completely idiosyncratic sort-of parody of the Japanese *tokusatsu* TV series ウルトラマン *Urutoraman / Ultraman* (originally broadcast 1966–67, though many spinoff series followed), brainchild of *Gojira/Godzilla* special effects creator Eiji Tsuburaya. I'd seen *Ultraman* during its first syndication appearance on Canadian television while growing up, so *Ultra Klutz* made perfect sense to me; it also appealed to the Toho monster movie lover in me, and the submerged childhood memories of silly superhero comics I had read in the barbershop. I also loved it as an aesthetic companion and successor of sorts to a long-forgotten underground comix one-shot, P. Serniuk's science-fiction gem *Mutants of the Metropolis* (1972). Nicholson later synopsized *Ultra Klutz* as the adventures of *"Sam Sogg [who] was just a lowly fast food worker on his home planet, but after crash landing on Earth, he is soon propelled to the status of hero. . . . Godzilla-like beasts begin sprouting up, and our former plebeian is fighting the good fight for mankind. . . . Part humor, part soap opera, it becomes intricate without taking itself too seriously. . ."* Jeff's crisp, uncluttered cartooning was perfectly suited to *Ultra Klutz*'s Tinkertoy universe, which evolved over the span of over 500 pages—31 issues and the capper *The Death of Ultra Klutz* (1992)—into something other than what it began as.

But—Jeff Nicholson in *Taboo?* Should I publish Jeff Nicholson's latest work alongside that of S. Clay Wilson, Rick Grimes, Charles Burns, Michael Zulli, Alejandro Jodorowsky, and Moebius, or Alan Moore and Eddie Campbell's *From Hell?* Could I really imagine the man behind *Ultra Klutz* having his work busted by Canadian, New Zealand, Australian, and British customs? The thought of the creator of *Ultra Klutz* being able to offer anything to *Taboo* seemed absurd, but the evidence was right there in my hands. I was blown away, forced to revise every impression I'd had of Nicholson's work up to that point. While *Ultra Klutz* heroically endured against all odds over the years of his publication, battling aliens and giant monsters and erratic sales, I doubt *Ultra Klutz* could have held his own against the genuine "monsters" lurking in the hallways and at the dark heart of *Habitrails*.

Through the Habitrails was a doorway into a world utterly foreign and alien, and yet terribly familiar, and all the more terrifying for its banality. It was the Court of the Gerbil King, and we have all, at one time or another, lived there (you may live there today). *Through the Habitrails* was an original—completely absorbing, and deeply, deeply disturbing. It was absolutely, genuinely Kafkaesque: as such, a way of seeing, rather than a description of what is seen.

Through the Habitrails was ideal for *Taboo.*

⟫◉⟪

Taboo had a very troubled history. Our (*Taboo* was co-founded with John Totleben, and initially co-edited with my then-wife Marlene O'Connor) goal, after all, was to

---

[12]The online edition of this collection is archived at http://fatherandsontoon.com/Tirade_contents.html

collect between covers the most disturbing comics stories and serialized graphic novels we could find, and that made *Taboo* a target for all manner of mischief and mishaps, not to mention Customs busts around the world. That's not important here, though all you need to know is that Jeff was one of the few creative individuals who used *Taboo* in the manner everyone who was part of that short-lived bastard experiment in "creator-friendly" publishing *should* have used it. Jeff seized the moment.

Jeff's series debuted in *Taboo* Vol. 5 (1991, SpiderBaby Grafix & Publications/ Tundra Publishing, Ltd.), and quickly became a fixture of the anthology. Indeed, Jeff was perhaps the only series creator published in *Taboo* who fully understood the rare opportunity the anthology provided. Once I accepted the *Through the Habitrails* initial installments for publication, Jeff hit the gas pedal and did not slow down until he was, to his satisfaction, finished with the entire series. The pay was humble by industry standards ($100 per page, with Jeff paying letterer Chad Woody out of his own pocket), but we were purchasing one-time only publishing rights only; the work remained the exclusive property of the creator(s). As editor, I did not in any way interfere with the creator or creation. When Jeff completed a chapter, I saw to it that the modest page rate was paid, and Jeff would already be hard at work on the next installment.

Though he completed his remarkable serialized graphic novel *Through the Habitrails* before the fatal final split between my publishing imprint SpiderBaby Grafix and our co-publisher Tundra, and was paid in full for all his completed work, the last few chapters never saw print in *Taboo*. Thereafter, all publishing rights reverted to Jeff, no strings attached (he gracefully permitted me to include the original, unrevised version of the chapter "Cat Lover" in *Taboo 8*, posthumously published by Kitchen Sink Press in 1995).

To this day, I'm amazed at Jeff's accomplishment. Not only was, and is, *Through the Habitrails* one of the seminal graphic novels of the 1990s, I still can't quite believe Jeff finished it amid the shambles *Taboo* and its co-publisher Tundra had become. Nicholson did not allow the spasms that rocked both *Taboo* and Tundra to impede or affect his own progress. His focus and goal remained absolute, a skill I admire even more in hindsight.

It's also essential to note Chad Woody's contribution to *Habitrails* as letterer. Nicholson was right to insist upon Woody lettering the entire serialized novel: Woody's lettering lent *Habitrails* its very distinctive "look," and (as we read lettering) "voice" (its absence was strongly felt in the lengthy chapter that Woody did *not* letter, "Cat Lover," which has been cut from this edition at Dover's request). At the time *Habitrails* was underway, Woody had blazed his own trails as a small-press cartoonist; Jeff was living and working in Chico, California, while Woody was based in the Ozarks, specifically Missouri. At the time, Woody was writing, drawing, and lettering his own comix for the Cranial Stomp minicomic imprint. The biography included in the 1994 *Bad Habit Habitrails* collected edition informed readers that Woody had "been involved in small press comix since age fifteen, when he started Cranial Stomp Comix with Brad Jones and other high school pals, publishing such titles as *Red Rogue, The Executioner's Son* and *El Toasterhead! Tales*," and that his "lettering on *Through the Habitrails* was his first published work outside of the small press . . ." Woody is still in Missouri, actively producing his mini-comics, and "publishing scattershots of poetry, comics, fiction, and printmaking on his own as well as in places like *The Iowa Review, Hayden's Ferry Review, Moon City Review,* and *Penthouse*. . . . he works in building maintenance" and recent projects "include *Junk Apocrypha,* a book collection of etchings, engravings, and woodcuts, and *Uncle Knuckle's Preposterous Narrations,* a bundle of absurd children's stories designed to blow all those celebrity-authored children's books to kingdom come"[13] as well as blogging ("Steadfastly Unsuccessful for 20 Years and Counting") at http://cranialstomp.blogspot.com/

---

[13]Chad Woody bio at *Thought Catalog,* archived at http://thoughtcatalog.com/chad-woody/

Before he died, Franz Kafka attempted to destroy all that he had written. He instructed his friend Max Brod to "burn everything " and requested that his already published work "[not] be reprinted and handed down to posterity."

We can only imagine what agonies Brod went through to deliberately ignore Kafka's final request. Indeed, some may revile Brod for his decision. It is only because Brod chose to rescue what precious little remained of Kafka's extraordinary body of work that we today recognize Kafka as one of the twentieth century's most vital literary voices.

I don't wish to embarrass Jeff Nicholson by further straining the echoes of Kafka that reverberate through *Habitrails*. Unlike Kafka, Jeff has not elected to relegate his own work to obscurity. For that, as much as for the merit of his work, I applaud him.

That *Through the Habitrails* still exists, in some form—*this* form—for you to read while so many vital comics creations have been relegated to obscurity is due to Jeff Nicholson himself. In the wake of *Taboo*'s and *Tundra*'s collapse, Nicholson prepared his own definitive reprint collection of *Through the Habitrails;* much as he did during the turbulent Taboo and Tundra years, Jeff assumed full responsibility for seeing through his own efforts to completion.

Even as the dust settled around the graves of his series publishers and its noxious vehicle, Jeff brought his serialized novel to the non-genre anthology *One Eye Open, One Eye Closed* (Chisasmus Comics), but that anthology venue collapsed after only a couple of installments. Eager to remedy the situation—while making a number of revisions to the chapters that had seen print—Jeff reworked and restructured the material, and in February 1994 he self-published the complete *Through the Habitrails* (Bad Habit; 144 pages, ISBN #1-885047-00-2). Nicholson revised *Habitrails* further for a second edition two years later, sporting a new laminated cover and fresh Epilogue (and an introduction by yours truly; 1996, Bad Habit, ISBN #1-885047-03-7).

And the Gerbil King laughed.

Despite Nicholson's best efforts, the comic book and graphic novel Direct Sales market imploded that very year (1996). *Through the Habitrails* surfaced and sank with little fanfare, a mere ripple in the maelstrom of the comic industry. Here was yet further evidence of the peculiar validity of Nicholson's not-entirely-invented *Habitrails* world: What had once been a viable system of production, distribution, and retail had been terminally undermined and infested with voracious, greedy deficiencies, dependencies, and opportunists. The efforts of countless creative individuals were habitually tapped and drained with terrifying speed, vital "juice" siphoned off in a mad feeding frenzy at the whim of yet another batch of unseen "superiors." Once again, Nicholson was in the Court of the Gerbil King, a mere microcosm of the grim realities of "doing business"in the corporate world dancing at the edge of the millennial abyss.

Still, Nicholson continued to work.[14]

A one-shot follow-up of sorts to Jeff's novel surfaced at DC Comics, of all places. Vertigo's *The Dreaming* #15 (August, 1997) showcased Jeff's full-color story "Day's Work, Night's Rest," a compelling self-sufficient tale and an excellent companion chapter to *Through the Habitrails*.

---

[14]After completing *Through the Habitrails* in 1994, Jeff Nicholson continued to produce comics series and serialized graphic novels, including the dark *Ultra Klutz* follow-up *Lost Laughter* (3 issues, 1993–94, concluded in a trio of serialized chapters in *Negative Burn*), the Eisner Award nominated ("Best Limited Series") *Father & Son* (4 issues and *Father & Son Like, Special #1*, 1994–98), the serialized "No Regrets" in *Negative Burn* #30--6 (1996, archived online at http://fatherandsontoon.com/No_Regrets1.html), the ambitious fantasy-adventure *Colonia* (11 issues, 1998-2005), and more. I particularly recommend *Colonia*, which was collected into two trade paperback editions by AiT/PlanetLAR. He has also returned to *Father & Son* for a series of web animation shorts (2007¬–2013).

The tone, texture, and narrative substance of Jeff's script and art were absolutely consistent with *Habitrails*, while fitting very comfortably into Neil Gaiman's *Sandman* (from which The Dreaming series derived) and *The Dreaming*'s conceptual universe. As such, it's an extraordinary example of a creator's very personal vision finding a rare perch in a mainstream title. And yet . . .

In a personal letter to me accompanying a signed copy of *The Dreaming* #15, Nicholson thanked me again for my "hands off" editorial helming of *Through the Habitrails* during its *Taboo* run, noting that Vertigo/DC Comics editors had hardly given him the same free hand, requiring constant and time-consuming rewrites, redrawing, and revisions. Nevertheless, in his public assessment of the gig, Jeff later wrote, "the money was great . . . and all delays aside, I turned in some top notch work."[15]

He did indeed.

———◦◦◦———

For this definitive current edition of *Through the Habitrails*, Nicholson (working with editor Drew Ford) has once again reshaped the material.

Interested completists may wish to track down the original publication of all the components, but for the rest of you, here's a brief overview of a few of the changes Jeff has made over the years. I cite only those I consider of particular interest and value, intrinsic to my own experience over the years of *Habitrails*.

* One chapter has been dropped completely from this Dover edition, the chapter entitled "Cat Lover." This originally proved by far the most problematic chapter for Jeff to wrestle through, for a multitude of reasons. Whereas the fantasy elements of *Through the Habitrails* handled the most intimate of details with some element of metaphor, such was not the case of "Cat Lover," which was agonizingly transparent in its confessional elements—hence, I suspect, the reason it proved the most difficult of all *Habitrails* chapters for Nicholson personally.

"Cat Lover" detailed the protagonist's strained relationship, from high school to adulthood, with the titular female character, a woman absolutely bound to her cats. This strained relationship led to their living together for a period of time, during which their already frayed relations stretched to the breaking point. The violence (directed primarily against cats) was vivid, making it all the more troubling a read; also, Nicholson lettered the entire chapter himself, which graphically set it apart from the rest of *Habitrails*, which had been lettered by Chad Woody.

"Cat Lover" was originally intended as the penultimate chapter of *Habitrails*, and it was eventually published in two forms:

—Jeff's original, unexpurgated version, which appeared complete in *Taboo 8*;

—Jeff's revised chapter, which became the longest chapter of both Bad Habit editions of *Habitrails*—positioned after "The Infiltrator" and before "Escape #3: Concow"—which was itself comprised of a prologue, four "chapters" within the chapter, and an epilogue, "I Scream for Ice Cream."

It was, in the final novel, no longer the penultimate chapter, comprising the central passage of both editions. The changes from the original version (which appeared in Taboo 8) involved cutting completely six pages of material (pages 16–21 of the original version), with extensive changes to the subsequent three pages (which became pages 17–19). Nicholson then extensively revised the epilogue, "I Scream for Ice Cream" (pages 26–29 of the version published in *Taboo 8*, pages 23–24 of the Bad Habit editions' revised chapter).

In short, the very elements that made "Cat Lover" a perfect fit for a confrontational adult horror anthology like *Taboo* seemed to usurp the flow and integrity of

---

[13]Chad Woody bio at *Thought Catalog*, archived at http://thoughtcatalog.com/chad-woody/

the definitive collected *Through the Habitrails*. Nicholson readily agreed with Dover's request to remove the chapter, and his decision stands.

* The 1996 revised Bad Habit edition of *Through the Habitrails* featured an explanatory, partially illustrated text epilogue by Nicholson. It read as both epilogue and confessional, further blurring the author's stated separation of himself from his work. As with Jeff's original introductory text (titled "No End" in this edition), I consider this relevant to those wishing to divine how much of *Habitrails* might be fueled by memoir, and how much might be metaphoric fantasy (the very process Nicholson specifically asked readers to resist).

Nicholson concluded, "This story could easily rate its own novella," a sequel entitled "The Whirling Nothing." But Nicholson had no intention of spending another "three years of my life chronicling the past three." The time-consuming realities of producing graphic novels is too often overlooked by those who've never tried or completed such a work.

Nevertheless, Nicholson offered an optimistic grace note: "I've learned through this experience that despondency can be swept away by the unexpected, and that joy can be torpedoed by same, yet I'm somehow not simply back where I started."

How can I help but wonder anew about how autobiographical *Through the Habitrails* might have been when Jeff concludes, "Don't worry. I'm not going back to the company. Perhaps I'll go out and find you another story."

≈∘≈

No doubt Jeff will bring you up to snuff on these and other matters in his own Afterword to this collected edition—or maybe not. Suffice it to note that he has "quit comics forever" at least a few times, as have we all at one time or another.

Well, hell, Jeff—here we are, back together again between two covers. It keeps on happening, doesn't it?

Somewhere, the Gerbil King is laughing still.

Jeff persevered, knowing that if he didn't see through the publication of *Through the Habitrails*, no one would.

I, for one, am thankful Jeff did so.

I'm even more thankful that Jeff has seen fit to work with Dover Publications to bring his novel back into print.

Jeff knows, in his heart of hearts, that *Through the Habitrails* is worth keeping in reach and alive in the world.

Forever.

But remember:

Never on Monday.

Stephen R. Bissette
© October 2015
Mountains of Madness, VT

CONTENTS

THROUGH THE
HABITRAILS

Life Before and After My Career in the Cubicles

INCREASING

THE GERBILS

~

Story and Illustration
Jeff Nicholson

Lettering
Chad Woody

©1990 Jeff Nicholson

WE LIVED IN A HOUSE TO THE RIGHT OF OUR WORKPLACE.

AN EARLIER STAFF HAD LIVED THERE WITHIN THE OFFICES, BUT IT WAS FELT SUCH PROXIMITY TO THE WORK AREA WAS UNHEALTHY.

FROM SECOND FLOOR PRODUCTION, YOU COULD SEE A BIT OF A VIEW THROUGH THE SIDE OF THE LARGE, ENERGY SAVING WINDOW-BLOCKS. SOME TREE LIFE COULD BE SEEN DIRECTLY FROM MY DESK.

CLEANLINESS AND POLISH WERE NOT REQUIRED OF OUR SURROUNDINGS, SO LONG AS WE COMPLETED OUR TASKS WITH REASONABLE QUALITY.

OURS WAS A PROGRESSIVE CORPORATION.

1.

1

WE WERE CONSTANTLY REMINDED OF OUR STATION IN LIFE BY THE GERBILS, WHICH EXISTED THROUGHOUT THE BUILDING IN A VAST COMPLEX OF CLEAR TUBES AND GREY, UNKEMPT TIN CAGES.

THE GERBILS WERE A LIVING SYMBIOSIS BETWEEN OUR EMPLOYERS AND OURSELVES. WHILE THEY REMINDED US OF THE FUTILITY OF LIFE OUTSIDE THE COMPANY, THEY WERE ALSO RELEASED REGULARLY FOR THE BENEFIT OF THE STAFF. AFTER YEARS OF SUCH SPECIALIZED DOMESTICATION THEY HAD BECOME EMPATHS OF STRESS AND DESPAIR.

THE GERBILS WOULD ATTEMPT TO FLEE, AND DISPLAY UNCONTROLLED CRINGING AND SCHIZOPHRENIA. THE DESTRUCTION OF GERBILS WAS NOT FROWNED UPON, AS THEIR LIFE SPAN WITHIN THE OFFICE WOULD NOT EXCEED THREE WEEKS DUE TO THE BOMBARDMENT OF MISERY. THE GERBIL INDUSTRY WAS MASSIVE, AND THE SUPPLY COULD ALWAYS BE INCREASED.

2.

IT WAS KNOWN THAT INTER-OFFICE ROMANCE WAS UNWISE, BUT CONTACT WITH THE GREATER CITY WAS BRIEF AND SUPER-FICIAL. WE WOULD FORM LOVE AFFAIRS WHICH WOULD QUICKLY CRASH TO A HALT OR DISSOLVE INTO EMPTINESS. THE SUPPLY OF GERBILS WOULD BE INCREASED.

DRUGS WERE ALLOWED, BUT WE WERE DETERRED FROM HEAVY ADDICTION. WE WERE ENCOURAGED TO INDULGE IN OUR DRUG NOT-OF-CHOICE. AS AN ALCOHOLIC, I WOULD SMOKE MARIJUANA IN THE EVENINGS, TO GIVE MYSELF SOME FORM OF ALTERATION WITHOUT DESTROYING MYSELF ON LIQUOR.

I DIDN'T ENJOY THE HIGH, WHICH CREATED A NEW FORM OF STRESS, BUT THE SUPPLY OF GERBILS COULD ALWAYS BE INCREASED.

I WAS ALLOWED MY DRUG IN EXTREME SITUATIONS. WHEN DEADLINES WERE SEVERE AND THE BUDGET LOW, I WOULD BE ADMINISTERED ONE SHOT OF GIN PER ILLUSTRATION PRODUCED AS INCENTIVE.

BUT THE ADMINISTRATOR'S TIME WAS BEST SPENT ELSEWHERE, SO A DEVICE WAS FASHIONED TO DELIVER MY DOSAGE AUTO-MATICALLY, TRIGGERED BY THE PASSAGE OF A GERBIL THROUGH THE TUBE.

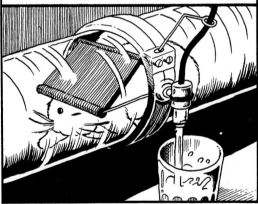

I SPENT MORE TIME TRYING TO COAX THE GERBILS TO SCURRY ALONG THE TUBE THAN ACTUALLY ILLUSTRATING, SO THIS INCENTIVE PLAN WAS ABANDONED.

ONE OF MY CO-WORKERS CONTINUED USING HIS DRUG OF CHOICE, LSD, EVEN WHILE ON THE JOB. HE CLAIMED AFTER THREE DAYS IN A ROW HE NO LONGER FELT ANY EFFECT AND CONTINUED ONE DOSE PER DAY FOR SEVERAL WEEKS, APPARENTLY UNALTERED.

HE BEGAN SLEEPING THERE IN THE OFFICE RATHER THAN IN THE HOUSE.

I COULD NOT ENDURE THE HOUSE MYSELF ONE NIGHT AFTER DISCOVERING A LOVE-QUADRANGLE, AND RETURNED TO THE BUILDING IN THE EARLY HOURS OF THE MORNING.

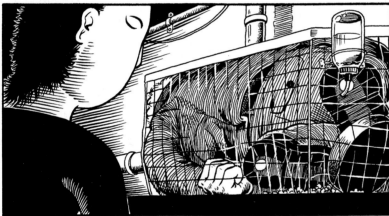

OVER NIGHT MY CO-WORKER HAD SOMEHOW COMPRESSED HIMSELF INTO ONE OF THE TIN CAGES. HE SEEMED ONLY REMOTELY AWARE OF HIS SURROUNDINGS, AND HAD LOST THE ABILITY TO SPEAK ANY WORKABLE LANGUAGE.

HE WAS RETAINED BY THE COMPANY AS A SURROGATE GERBIL, AND LIVED FAR BEYOND THE EXPECTED THREE WEEKS.

END.

4

IT'S NOT YOUR JUICE

©1990 Jeff Nicholson

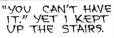 Story and Illustration: Jeff Nicholson ~ Lettering: Chad Woody

"IT ISN'T YOURS," I FUTILELY THOUGHT AS I RETURNED TO SECOND FLOOR PRODUCTION.

"YOU CAN'T HAVE IT." YET I KEPT UP THE STAIRS.

AT LUNCH I GOT MAIL THAT GAVE ME JUICE. I JUST WANTED TO TAKE IT HOME. USE IT SPARINGLY ON SOMETHING WONDERFUL.

THE SALES PEOPLE BEGAN TAPPING ME RIGHT AWAY.

THEIR TAPS ARE SMALL, BUT THE JUICE RUNS THROUGH THEM QUICKER THAN THE LARGER ONES.

I CAN NEVER SEE WHO IT IS WHO DOES MY TEMPLE.

IT DOESN'T DRAIN TERRIBLY FAST. I JUST FIND IT INSULTING.

AT NIGHT I DRINK A DIFFERENT JUICE TO SEAL THE PUNCTURES.

WHILE THAT WHICH WAS TAKEN FROM ME IS FED TO THE GERBILS.

BUT THAT'S A DIFFERENT STORY...

NO END

I ENJOY DOING THE THINGS THAT I'M DOING BUT I DON'T WANT TO RISK LOSING THE PLEASURE OF DOING THEM BY FINISHING THEM. I'M YOUNG AND I HAVE TO DO SOME OF THESE THINGS WHILE I'M STILL YOUNG (THERE'S SO MANY OTHER THINGS I COULD DO AS AN OLD MAN). BUT THEN I WANT TO DO THOSE THINGS I COULD DO AS AN OLD MAN NOW BECAUSE THEY MAY NOT BE OF INTEREST TO ME IN THE FUTURE. BUT I DON'T WANT TO FINISH THEM. I DON'T WANT THE PLEASURE TO END. I WANT THEM TO BE THERE ALWAYS. I WANT TO KNOW THE PLEASURE IS ALWAYS WAITING. AND ALL THE WHILE I DO THESE THINGS THAT I CREATE AND MANIPULATE, I'M MISSING THE NATURAL THINGS. THE LAND AND TRAVELLING AND LOVE AND JUST DOING NOTHING. BUT IF I STOP AND DO THE NATURAL THINGS I JUST KEEP THINKING ABOUT THE OTHER THINGS TO THE POINT OF NOT REALLY ENJOYING THE NATURAL THINGS. THERE ARE SO MANY OF THESE THINGS THEY OVERWHELM ME. THEY HURT MY BRAIN AND I HAVE TO STOP. BUT THEN I'M NOT DOING THEM OR ENJOYING THEM ANYMORE. I TRY TO DIG IN AND GET SOMETHING DONE SO I CAN GET ON TO THE NEXT THING, BUT THEN I'M RUSHING IT. I'VE FINISHED IT AND I'VE FAILED TO EXPERIENCE THE PLEASURE I PROMISED I WOULD GAIN FROM IT.

6

JAR HEAD

~

Story and Illustration
Jeff Nicholson

Lettering
Chad Woody

THE ACT OF DRINKING BEER BECAME CUMBERSOME, AND I DRANK IN SUCH QUANTITY, THAT IT BECAME MUCH MORE PRACTICAL TO FASHION A LARGE PICKLE JAR AROUND MY HEAD.

AT FIRST I WOULD FILL IT TO JUST BELOW MY NOSE, TO DRINK AND BREATHE IN HARMONY. IN SECOND FLOOR PRODUCTION, THIS BEHAVIOR WAS VIEWED WITH ONLY MILD AMUSEMENT.

IN TIME, THE AIR SEEMED LESS IMPORTANT, AND THE CARBONATION FROM THE BEER WAS ENOUGH TO SUSTAIN ME.

1.

EVENINGS AT HOME SAW MORE WORK, MY OWN SELF-IMPOSED INDUSTRIOUS VIGIL. THE WORK WAS MINE TO ENJOY, BUT WITH THE HANDICAP OF HAVING BEEN TAPPED BY THE DAY. THE COMPANY WON TWO-THIRDS OF MY LIFE, AND DRAINED THE JUICES FROM MY DRIVEN FLESH FOR ITS OWN NEEDLESS PRODUCT.

THE JAR WAS KEPT FULL. I COULD EASILY WORK ON MY PROJECTS IN THIS STATE OF INCREASING DRUNKENNESS, BY DOING TASKS OF DECREASING COMPLEXITY AS THE NIGHT PROGRESSED.

WHEN COORDINATION WAS BEYOND ME, I SLIPPED INTO THE FINAL HOUR. A WARM, SAFE CAPSTONE TO MY DAY. RECREATION. SUSTENANCE. OBLIVION.

2.

8

AS I SAID, I USED CAUTION AT SOME POINT IN THE PAST. WHEN FIRST HIRING ON WITH THE CORPORATION, I THINK. IT'S HARD TO REMEMBER. I LET THE JAR RUN NEARLY OUT BY THE END OF THE NIGHT. NO NEED FOR EXCESSIVE BEHAVIOR.

IN THE MORNING, THE LEVEL HAD EVAPORATED DOWN. THE SMELL OF THE REMAINING WARM, FLAT BEER, AND THE REQUIREMENT TO USE MY LUNGS AGAIN, WAS AN UGLY SHOCK TO MY SYSTEM.

SOMETIMES I TOYED WITH THE IDEA OF GETTING RID OF THE JAR ALL TOGETHER, UNTIL I STUMBLED UPON A FANTASTIC BIO-BOOZE PHENOMENON...

IF I WENT TO SLEEP WITH THE JAR ALMOST FULL, MY HEAD WOULD BECOME, IN A SENSE, PICKLED.

THE FOLLOWING DAY I FELT FINE. LIKE A DEAD FROG IN FORMALDEHYDE, MY HEAD COULD JUST FLOAT IN THE FLUID, REQUIRING NO INTAKE OF AIR **OR** BEER. THE WORLD WAS DULL AND BLURRY, BUT I COULD EASILY WORK FOR THE COMPANY (AND ITS LIMITED STANDARDS FOR CREATIVITY) IN THIS STATE.

3.

BY AFTERNOON THE OLD, FLAT BEER WOULD EVAPORATE BELOW MY NOSE, BUT THE SHOCK WAS LESS SEVERE. A BIT OF COMMON SENSE TOLD ME TO START KEEPING IT COMPLETELY FULL THAT NIGHT.

IT WORKED! THE DANK FLUID NEVER EVAPORATED. EVERY EVENING ABOUT SIX, I JUST DUMPED OUT THE OLD STUFF AND REFILLED IT WITH FRESH BREW, TO MAINTAIN THE PICKLING.

I ONLY VOICED RESISTANCE DURING THIS BRIEF TRANSITION, BUT BY THEN MY BODY WAS COMPLETELY DIVORCED FROM MY LOGICAL MIND.

IT SEEMS MY RIGHT BRAIN HAD SWOLLEN TO TEN TIMES THE SIZE OF MY DIMINISHED LEFT BRAIN.

AND THE BEAUTY OF THE PROCESS PRESENTED ITSELF TO ME.

THE FULL JAR **GAVE** ME JUICE. IT KEPT ME UP LONG INTO THE NIGHT. LIKE A SECRET BIOLOGY EXPERIMENT, I SLEPT LESS AND LESS EACH NIGHT.

I COULD FUNCTION FINE IN THE MORNING, BUT WHEN THEY TAPPED ME, NOTHING CAME OUT. NOW THE BASTARDS ONLY HAD HALF MY LIFE.

I HAD THE STRONG TIME. THE FRESH START. A FULL SHIFT TO USE **MY** JUICE ON **MY** WORK. I HAD COMPLETELY TURNED THE TABLES ON THEM. MY LIFE WAS MINE TO COMMAND. THE LEFTOVER WASTE SLUFFED OFF ON THEM.

5.

11

EVERYTHING SEEMED SO IDEALISTIC. SO SAFE IN THIS WARM POND.

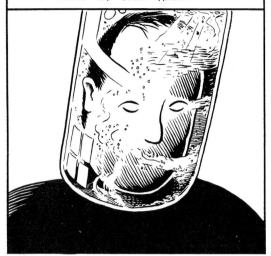

UNTIL THE BAD THINGS HAPPENED. THE BAD BODY THINGS.

IT STARTED WITH THE KNIVES. ESPECIALLY RAZOR BLADES. TO LOOK AT THEM I COULD FEEL THE CUTTING. I COULD FEEL I WAS MEAT.

WHEN I DREW, MY HANDS SHOOK. TO USE THEM FELT UNNATURAL. MY WRISTS PIVOTED LIKE MECHANICAL PROTOTYPES OF WHAT WRISTS SHOULD BE.

I WONDERED IF THEY WERE ASKING TO BE CUT. MY BODY WAS A DRY HUSK. I IMAGINED A MAROON RED POWDER WOULD HAVE COME OUT, HAD I GONE THROUGH WITH IT.

ON MY LATE WALKS I THOUGHT OF BODIES FIGHTING. MUSCLE BRUISING LIKE MEAT LEFT OUT ON THE COUNTER TOO LONG. SMELLING BAD.

BEFORE THE JAR, EXERCISE KEPT MY SYSTEM VITAL. I HAD TO STOP EVEN ATTEMPTING IT, FOR THE FLUSH, ILL FEELING IT GAVE ME.

I KNEW IT WAS CORRECT TO EAT, AND FOOD TASTED GOOD, BUT FROM THE THROAT DOWN IT FELT LIKE A HARD, RUSTY INFESTATION.

I CAN'T ALLOW THE THOUGHT OF INFESTATION. FAR WORSE THAN KNIVES ARE THE PARASITES. I HATE THE THOUGHT.

MY BODY BECAME A HONEY-COMBED MASS WHICH SERVED MY PURPOSES, BUT SEEMED BOTH UNFAMILIAR AND FRIGHTENING.

THERE COULD BE EGGS THERE.

7.

13

I USED DARKER ALES AND MALTS.

IT BECAME DIFFICULT TO DISTINGUISH REALITY FROM THE ODD REFLECTIONS THAT DARTED THROUGH THIS DARK, SEPIA LIQUID.

I BECAME COMPLETELY DISORIENTED, PACING WITH EMOTIONAL HALLUCINATIONS.

MY LIMBS WOULD MAKE SUDDEN MOVES OF THEIR OWN WILL.

THE LIGHT CAST THROUGH THE GLASS AND BLACK BEER IN JUST SUCH A WAY, THAT AN IMAGE APPEARED ON THE INSIDE, DIRECTLY IN FRONT OF MY FACE

IT WAS VAGUE.

IT MADE NO SENSE.

IT WAS MY REFLECTION.

IT SCARED THE HELL OUT OF ME.

8.

END.

14

THE DOOMED ONE

THE DOOMED ONE SAT.

SHE DEVOURED HER WORK AS INTENSELY AS SHE MUST HAVE DEVOURED FOOD, BUT WITH AN **ANGRY** INTENSITY. SHE HATED EACH JOB GIVEN HER, SO PERHAPS SHE ALSO HATED THE BODY SHE CORRUPTED WITH EXCESS FOOD.

WE ALL KNEW OUR WORK WAS DEPRESSING, BUT FOR SURVIVAL REASONS, A RESISTANCE WAS BUILT UP TO IT. AFTER ENOUGH YEARS, A DAY OF FRUSTRATING, UNWANTED TASKS WAS JUST ANOTHER DAY OF SAME.

©1990 Jeff Nicholson

WE ENDURED IT UNDER A SHELL OF PLAYFUL SARCASM, AND A KNOWLEDGE THAT IT WAS JUST THE COMPANY'S USELESS PRODUCT. IT WOULD ALL GET DONE EVENTUALLY.

JARHEAD BAR & GRILL

STANLEY WEBER IS WATCHING

THE DOOMED ONE, HOWEVER, WOULD BE CONSUMED WITH RAGE OVER THE MOST AVERAGE CONDITIONS.

SALES REPS UNFORTUNATE ENOUGH TO BRING HER JOBS WOULD BE TREATED LIKE NAUGHTY CHILDREN OR COMPLETE INCOMPETENTS.

THEN SHE REGURGITATED HER COMPLAINTS TO EVERYONE AROUND HER. A HATRED WAS IN HER VOICE THAT WOULD TAKE A GRIP OF YOUR INNER ORGANS.

I COULDN'T MAKE SENSE OF IT. WHY WAS I FATED TO SIT NEXT TO THE DOOMED ONE?

I CAME IN EARLY TO WORK IN PEACE, BUT ULTIMATELY SHE WOULD ARRIVE, AND UNRAVEL THE REMAINDER OF MY SANITY.

2.

16

IT ADDED DESPAIR TO AN ALREADY FUTILE ENVIRONMENT BECAUSE...

THE DOOMED ONE WOULD NOT LEAVE.

I FIRST SAW THE DOOMED ONE DURING A COLLEGE TOUR, LONG BEFORE HIRING ON WITH THE COMPANY.

PERCHED IN THAT SAME CORNER, SHE WAS A BEACON OF FRUSTRATION AND MISERY.

I BEGAN TO QUESTION MY CAREER CHOICE.

I FOUND MYSELF SERVING AN INTERN-SHIP WITH THE COMPANY A YEAR LATER. I WAS FORTUNATE ENOUGH TO BE SERVING UNDER SOMEONE OTHER THAN THE DOOMED ONE.

I WATCHED AS A CLASSMATE SUFFERED UNDER HER TORTUROUS TUTELAGE. AS EARLY AS 8:00 AM SHE BEGAN WORRYING ABOUT WHERE TO GO FOR LUNCH.

3.

YEARS AFTER MY INTERNSHIP, I WAS HIRED BY THE COMPANY. MOST OF THE FACES HAD CHANGED, BUT THE DOOMED ONE STILL SAT, IN QUIET FUROR.

MY DESK SAT WAITING BESIDE.

UNLIKE MYSELF, WHOSE MOODS AND ANGERS WERE SUBDUED LIKE A SLOW BURNING CANDLE, HER MANNERISMS WERE LIKE A LIGHT SWITCH. HER INSTANT TANTRUMS JUST AS QUICKLY COOLED BACK DOWN, WHILE I WAS LEFT WITH A SLOW BURN OF FRUSTRATION OVER HER OUTBURSTS.

I COULDN'T DECIDE IF HER MOMENTS OF JOY WERE MORE UNNERVING THAN HER HATRED. SHE SPOKE WITH A TWISTED PRIDE OVER HER IMPORTANCE TO THE COMPANY. SHE WAS EAGER TO DISPLAY HER USELESS KNOWLEDGE; TO OFFER OPINIONS; TO BLUNDER THROUGH CONVERSATIONS UNINVITED.

I JUST WANTED TO ESCAPE.

WORKERS NEWER AND YOUNGER THAN THE DOOMED ONE HAD LONG SINCE BEEN PROMOTED TO THE "FUN HOUSE," A DEPARTMENT WHERE WORK WAS SLIGHTLY LESS DEMEANING.

4.

18

NEXT TO FOOD, THE DOOMED ONE SPOKE MOSTLY OF HER FUTURE. IN THE INNER CITY, SHE WOULD SOON HIRE ON WITH THE **BIG** CORPORATION. SHE NEEDED ONLY TIME IN HER HECTIC LIFESTYLE TO FINISH HER PORTFOLIO.

IT WAS DIFFICULT TO IMAGINE HER LIFE OUTSIDE THE COMPANY. SHE HAD A GAUNT, LIFELESS BOYFRIEND, DROVE A VEHICLE FILLED WITH FAST FOOD WASTE, AND MAINTAINED LARGE DOGS.

EVENTUALLY ANOTHER POSITION IN THE FUN HOUSE OPENED UP, DUE TO AN EMOTIONAL SETBACK BY ONE OF THE DESIGNERS.

THIS CO-INCIDED WITH THE DOOMED ONE'S CRASH SELF-IMPROVEMENT COURSE FOR HER 5-YEAR SERVITUDE AWARD.

SHE WAS EAGER TO BE PHOTOGRAPHED FOR WHAT THE COMPANY CALLED THE "HALL OF FAME," TO BE IMMORTAL-IZED IN A PLAQUE. THOSE IN THE LOWER LEVELS REFERRED TO IT AS THE "WALL OF SHAME."

SHE BOUGHT A FUN OUTFIT, DID HER HAIR, AND EVEN LOST WEIGHT (BUT TALKED ABOUT FOOD FOUR TIMES AS MUCH IN THE PROCESS).

AT OFFICE PARTIES SHE TALKED OF HER OPTIONS. POSSIBILITIES IN THE INNER CITY COULD COMPLETELY OVERSHADOW THE NEW FUN HOUSE POSITION. IT WAS TIME TO SEVER ROOTS AND GO FOR THE BIG MONEY. SHE WAS RATHER FRIGHTENING ON ALCOHOL.

THE FUN HOUSE POSITION WAS GIVEN TO THE YOUNG- EST, MOST RECENTLY EMPLOYED MEMBER OF THE STAFF.

THE DOOMED ONE ARRIVED DRUNK THE NEXT DAY, SPITTING FIRE AT ANYONE WHO GOT NEAR.

THE GERBILS, BRED AS EMPATHS FOR DESPAIR BY THE COMPANY, BEGAN SWARMING AT AN ALARMING RATE.

THEY FED OFF OUR MISERY, BUT WERE NOT ACCUSTOMED TO SUCH DIRECT AND DECISIVE ANGER.

6.

SOME SWARMED TOWARDS HER, SOME RAN AWAY. SO MUCH SCURRYING FUR BROUGHT THE TENSION TO MAXIMUM.

SHE DESTROYED ALL SHE COULD GET HER HANDS ON, AND AFTER VANDALIZING PART OF THE HABITRAIL SYSTEM, WAS SENT HOME.

THAT NIGHT I SAW HER IN THE MARKET BUYING FOUR TWIN PACKS OF DIP CHIPS AND SEVERAL KINDS OF COOKIES.

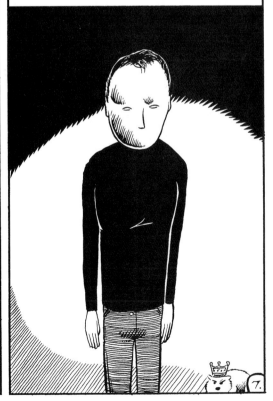

THEN CAME MY EXIT FROM THE COMPANY. THAT'S A DIFFERENT STORY.

7.

21

YEARS LATER I DELIVERED SOME MATERIALS TO THE CORPORATION. IT FELT STRANGE TO SEE THAT OLD PLACE AGAIN.

ON MY WAY OUT, I FOLLOWED A GROUP OF STUDENTS TOURING THE BUILDING. IT WAS HARD TO IMAGINE MYSELF AS ONE OF THOSE YOUNG PEOPLE, UNSURE OF WHICH DIRECTION LIFE WOULD TAKE.

TWO OF THEM MUTTERED SOMETHING ABOUT GETTING OUT OF DESIGN, GESTURING TOWARDS ACROSS THE ROOM.

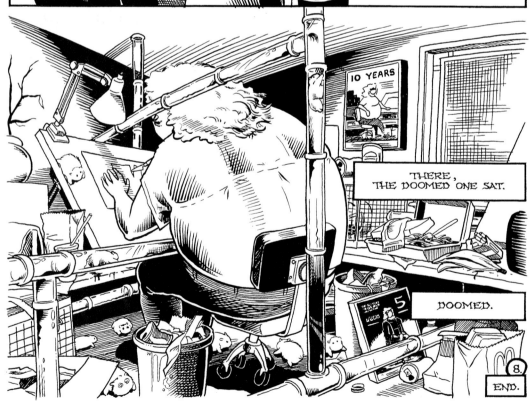

10 YEARS

THERE, THE DOOMED ONE SAT.

DOOMED.

8.

END.

ESCAPE #1: "EL MUERTE"

MY JOB. MY HOME. MY FRIENDS. MY
CO-WORKERS. ALL THE ROOMS IN
ALL THE BUILDINGS IN THE CITY.
IT WOULD ALL BECOME A BLUR,
AND I HAD TO ESCAPE.

©1990 Jeff Nicholson

I KNEW EVERY MOVE I WOULD MAKE.
EACH JOB I WOULD COMPLETE.
EVERYTHING I WOULD CREATE.
WHEN AND HOW I WOULD DO WHAT
I LOVED AND HATED, AND I HAD TO ESCAPE.

I WOKE UP AND THOUGHT
OF ALL THE THINGS I'D BEEN ACHING TO DO
ON MY DAY OFF, AND I DISCARDED THOSE
THOUGHTS. I HAD TO ESCAPE INTO
COMPLETELY UNEXPECTED STIMULATION.
I WENT TO THE CEMETERY.

IT WAS AN OLD AND
BEAUTIFUL PLACE. I
DIDN'T UNDERSTAND WHY
MORE PEOPLE DIDN'T GO THERE.
THE IDEA OF HUNDREDS OF
DEAD PEOPLE WAS FASCINATING.

GARY
TETER

1

IT SEEMED ODD THAT THE TREES AND GRASS WERE A BENEFIT FOR THE DEAD. COULDN'T WE GIVE THEM THE BUILDINGS TO PILE UP IN WHILE WE LIVED OUT HERE?

I COULDN'T IMAGINE THESE DEAD PEOPLE WERE REALLY ALL THAT SAD TO BE DEAD.

I BROUGHT MY CAMERA. DURING MY ESCAPE, I COULDN'T DO THE THINGS I NORMALLY DID, SO I PICKED PHOTOGRAPHY. A TOTALLY FOREIGN MEDIUM.

I LOVED THE WAY THE LIGHT CAME IN THROUGH THE TREES AND TOMBSTONES.

THE EERINESS OF THE STACKED CEMENT MAUSOLEUM CASKETS HIDDEN IN THE BACK.

AN OLD ROAD WITH DENSE TREES. IT REMINDED ME OF THE "SCARY" PART OF THE YELLOW BRICK ROAD.

2.

24

I DROVE UP TO THE FOOTHILLS, WHERE I KNEW AN OLD REST STOP HAD BEEN DISMANTLED BY THE STATE A FEW YEARS AGO.

I LOVED IMAGES OF EROSION. MAN MADE THINGS FALLEN INTO DECAY. AS A BOY I HAD VIVID DAYDREAMS OF BEING ALONE IN A POST~NUCLEAR LANDSCAPE.

THERE WERE MORE GREAT IMAGES HERE. ROADS CRACKED WITH WEEDS TAKING OVER.

PARTIAL FENCES THAT FENCED NOTHING.

AND THE BEST: A SOLITARY HIGHWAY REFLECTOR STANDING IN A FIELD OF DEAD GRASS.

THEN I FOUND SOMETHING UNEXPLAINABLE. PLASTIC TRASH BAGS FILLED WITH BONES.

SEVERAL OF THEM.

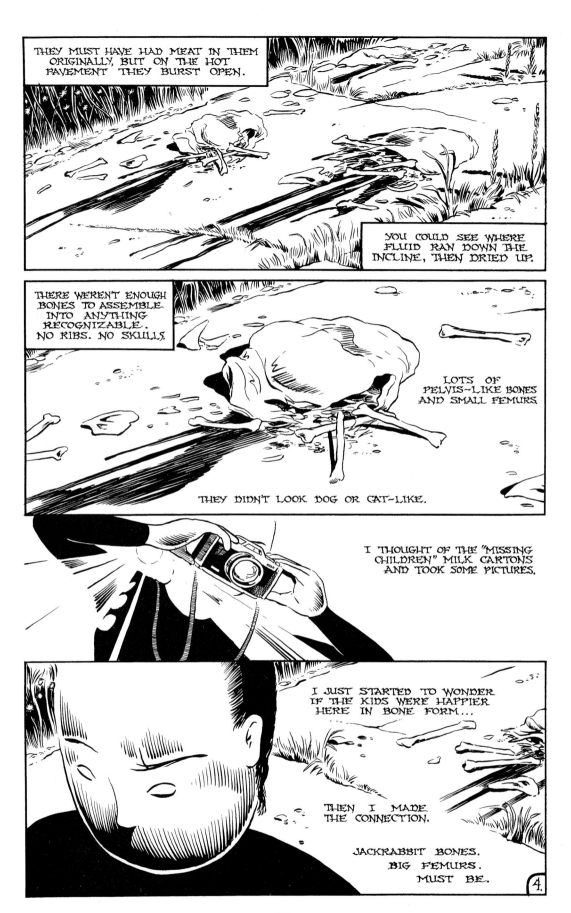

THEY MUST HAVE HAD MEAT IN THEM ORIGINALLY, BUT ON THE HOT PAVEMENT THEY BURST OPEN.

YOU COULD SEE WHERE FLUID RAN DOWN THE INCLINE, THEN DRIED UP.

THERE WEREN'T ENOUGH BONES TO ASSEMBLE INTO ANYTHING RECOGNIZABLE. NO RIBS. NO SKULLS.

LOTS OF PELVIS~LIKE BONES AND SMALL FEMURS.

THEY DIDN'T LOOK DOG OR CAT-LIKE.

I THOUGHT OF THE "MISSING CHILDREN" MILK CARTONS AND TOOK SOME PICTURES.

I JUST STARTED TO WONDER IF THE KIDS WERE HAPPIER HERE IN BONE FORM...

THEN I MADE THE CONNECTION.

JACKRABBIT BONES. BIG FEMURS. MUST BE.

4.

BY THE END OF THE DAY I REACHED A PLACE WHERE MODERN HIGHWAYS REPLACED MOUNTAIN ROADS FROM DECADES AGO. COMPLETELY FORGOTTEN AND HIDDEN AWAY.

THERE I SAW THE BEST IMAGE. A ROAD TO NOWHERE. IT JUST TURNED TO RUBBLE. A PASSAGEWAY TO OBLIVION.

I FELL IN LOVE WITH IT.

BACK ON THE HIGHWAY I FOUND A DEAD CAT.

IT LAYED ON ITS SIDE FOR SO LONG THAT IT LOOKED LIKE A HALF A CAT.

I GOT AN EXCITING IDEA. USING HIDDEN STICKS AS PROPS, I TOOK SEVERAL PHOTOS OF THE DEAD CAT "JUMPING" IN AND OUT OF THE BUSHES. ITS FACE LOOKED HAUNTED.

THE SETTING SUN'S LIGHT LOOKED JUST LIKE THE MORNING RAYS AT THE CEMETERY

LATER I WOULD PUT THE PHOTOS TOGETHER FOR A "NIGHT OF THE LIVING DEAD KITTY" MONTAGE. 5.

WHEN I HAD THE FILM DEVELOPED, I FOUND OUT THE CAMERA I BORROWED WAS LOADED WITH SLIDE FILM INSTEAD OF PRINT FILM.

LATE INTO THE NIGHT, AFTER MUCH DRINKING, I THOUGHT OF A WAY TO PRESERVE MY ESCAPE IN THE FORM OF A SURREAL SLIDE SHOW.

BY NEARLY DAWN, MY MIND WAS IN HIGH GEAR. THE FLOW OF ALCOHOL GAVE ME A SWEET CREATIVE EDGE.

I TAPED A VOCAL NARRATIVE THAT WOULD ACCOMPANY THE SHOW.

I REARRANGED THE IMAGES IN AN ORDER THAT WAS LINEAR TO THE WAY I FELT ABOUT THEM, INSTEAD OF IN THE ACTUAL ORDER TAKEN.

MY ESCAPE WAS OVER. I HAD AN HOUR TO GET SOME SLEEP AND RETURN TO THE OFFICE.

IT WAS AMAZING HOW FAST I COULD RECUPERATE AT WORK. KEEPING THE JAR FULLER AT NIGHT WAS WORKING.

6.

I drove and drove, until the roads began to die. I had to leave the car and go on foot.

People have stumbled this way accidentally, but few came on purpose like I did.

Those who did try lay on the roadside. Their bodies failed them at that point.

I saw the last piece of civilization. I felt like I was really going to make it this time.

I could see it ahead. An ancient and beautiful place. So peaceful.

I was nearly there, then the light was obscured. Something unresolved was nagging at me.

Something hissing and horrible was there, heading me off through the bushes.

A cat! A mean, ugly, shrieking dead cat! I'm so much bigger but it scared me away.

Why was it ruining everything? It drove me down a dark passage to the side.

It mocked me and ran off. I hate cats that run away. I felt tricked and powerless.

It was too late. I could see signs of civilization again. A road grew out of the brush.

It led to my car. I had to go back. I'll have to get rid of some baggage before trying again.

I ALMOST FORGOT ABOUT THE SLIDE SHOW UNTIL AN OFFICE PARTY CAME UP. I THOUHT IT WOULD MAKE GREAT ENTERTAINMENT, AND HUSTLED MY EQUIPMENT TOGETHER.

I DISPLAYED MY SHOW, BRIMMING WITH ENTHUSIASM.

MANY LEFT BEFORE ITS COMPLETION.

MANY MORE AFTER THE ENDING, WITH NO COMMENT GIVEN.

THEY DIDN'T SEE THE EDGE. THEY DISMISSED MY ESCAPE AS SILLY. OR SCARY. BUT IT WAS NEITHER.

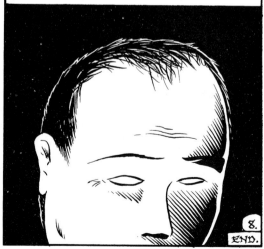

NEXT TIME, I WOULD HAVE TO ESCAPE FARTHER.

8. END.

30

Futile Love

©1991 Jeff Nicholson

SHE WOULD BE SO LOVELY, IF NOT FOR THE OVERSIZED PINK JACKET, AND THE LONG STRAIGHT HAIR.

BUT THEN, I DON'T TRY TO CHANGE PEOPLE. THAT'S A BIG MISTAKE IN LOVE.

BUT I DON'T MEAN TO SAY THAT I LOVE HER. I'M JUST INTRIGUED BY THE FACT THAT SHE HASN'T DISPLAYED ANY NEUROSES OR INSECURITIES YET.

LIKE ALL THE OTHERS...

1.

NOT THAT I CARE, REALLY. IT WOULD ONLY MATTER IF I THOUGHT OF THEM AS POTENTIAL LOVERS.

BUT I DON'T

I LIKE BEING ALONE.

IT'S ALL A CRUEL JOKE I HAVE TO ENDURE. DEEP INSIDE THERE'S AN ACHE TO BE LOVED. BUT TO BE INTIMATE WITH ANY OF THESE LUNATICS WOULD CAUSE MORE GRIEF THAN PLEASURE.

I THINK OF MY COLLEGE DAYS AND IT'S HARD TO BELIEVE THAT THAT WAS ME.

MY PHILOSOPHY WAS TO DIVE INTO ANY EXPERIENCE WITH ANYONE, JUST TO HAVE FELT IT, REGARDLESS OF ANY PAINFUL OUTCOME. EVERY GIRL IN THE WORLD WAS AN EXCITING, BEAUTIFUL POSSIBILITY.

THAT WAS BEFORE MY EXPERIENCE WITH THE ONE I CALL "CAT LOVER."

2.

NOW THERE IS NOTHING SO FASCINATING ABOUT WOMEN. THEIR FAULTS ARE SO GLARINGLY OBVIOUS. BEFORE I COULD EVEN MUSTER UP AN ATTRACTION TO THEM, THEY INSURE MY REVULSION.

THE TALL BLONDE ONE. SHE IS A PARASITE, JUST LIKE THE GERBILS IN THE WALLS. BUT THE GERBILS ARE PUT THERE BY THE CORPORATION. SHE SHOULD BE ON **MY** SIDE.

I COPE WITH THIS JOB WITH REBELLIOUS HUMOR. A BITTER CLASS CLOWN WITH THE D.T.s. I'M CHARMING AND GOOFY AND THE BLONDE ONE IS MY FRIEND.

BUT WHEN MY LIFE STABILIZES A BIT, I'M CONTENT TO JUST BE ALONE WITH MY THOUGHTS THROUGH THE DAY. THEN THE BLONDE ONE SEEMS IRRITATED THAT I'M NOT PERFORMING FOR HER.

COULD A MAN LIVE WITH SUCH DEMANDS? 3.

THE SHORT CURLY-HAIRED BRUNETTE.
FOREVER TRAPPED IN A HIGH-SCHOOLISH WORLD.
TO BE ETERNALLY "CUTE" IS HER CALLING IN LIFE.

TO AROUSE ME (OR TO ASTOUND THE STAFF?)
SHE SAYS TO ME OUT OF THE BLUE,
"WE NEED TO GET AWAY FOR A WEEK-END.
JUST RUN OFF AND HAVE SOME FUN!"

IN A FEW DAYS, BEFORE I CAN DETERMINE
THE SINCERITY OF IT, SHE IS REPEATING HER
PERFORMANCE FOR A NEW EMPLOYEE.

COULD A MAN LIVE WITH SUCH FAITHLESSNESS?

IT DOESN'T
MATTER.
MY
FANTASIES
GIVE ME
MUCH MORE
PLEASURE
THAN
ANY OF
THESE
LIVING,
BREATHING,
COMPLICATIONS
COULD.

4.

YET THERE'S THAT TYPESETTER...

SHE WOULD BE SO LOVELY, IF NOT FOR THE ENORMOUS GLASSES, AND WEAK CHIN.

BUT EVEN IF I WANTED SOMEONE, I REALIZE THE FOLLY OF INTER-OFFICE ROMANCE. WHEN IT GOES BAD, YOU'RE FORCED TO LIVE WITH YOUR MISTAKE DAILY.

WHICH I SUPPOSE IS WHAT MADE ME EVEN CONSIDER THE TEMPORARY GIRL.

SHE CAME UP FROM A DIFFERENT BRANCH TO ASSIST ON A BIG PROJECT. SHE WAS ATTRACTIVE, AND I FELT A SMALL RUSH OF THAT COLLEGE OPTIMISM.

SHE WAS WORKING WITH THE MANAGER ON SOMETHING. I DID AN ILLUSTRATION FOR IT, AND SHOWED IT TO HER, SAYING, "SHOULD I GIVE THIS TO YOU?"

SHE SAID, "YEAH. YOU CAN GIVE IT TO ME.

"AND THEN **I** CAN GIVE IT TO THE MANAGER. **OR** YOU CAN JUST GIVE IT TO THE MANAGER."

SHE COULDN'T SAY, "THANKS. THAT GOES TO THE MANAGER." OR SOMETHING.

COULD A MAN LIVE WITH SUCH POINTED SARCASM?

AT AN OFFICE PARTY THE TYPESETTER KEPT GRAVITATING TOWARDS ME. CONFIDING IN ME THE TRIALS OF BREAKING UP WITH HER BOYFRIEND.

I HAD TO WATCH MYSELF, NOT LET MYSELF GET SUCKED INTO A SITUATION JUST BECAUSE IT WAS THERE.

MAYBE SHE JUST NEEDED A FRIEND. HAVING NEVER CONFIDED WITH ANYONE ABOUT THE CAT LOVER, MAYBE I COULD USE A FRIEND TOO.

THE PARTY MADE ITS WAY BACK TO THE COMMUNAL HOUSE. LIKE MIGRANT FARMHANDS, THE CORPORATION OFFERED US LOW RENT HOUSING IN THE SURROUNDING BUILDINGS IT BOUGHT UP.

TO LIVE THERE WASN'T MANDATORY, BUT FOR FINANCIAL REASONS, WE DID. THE INTIMACY BLURRED OUR PERSONAL AND WORK RELATIONSHIPS. ANOTHER REASON NOT TO GET INVOLVED.

HER BOYFRIEND ROOMED WITH HER, AND WAS WAITING THERE FOR HER. A SMALL, SINISTER LOOKING FELLOW. SHE IGNORED HIM.

THEN, IN A BRAZEN, UNINHIBITED WAY (NOT AT ALL TYPICAL OF HER), SHE PREPARED US FOR AN ANNOUNCEMENT.

6.

36

THE ODD LITTLE EX-BOYFRIEND GAVE HER A FIXED GLARE OF DISAPPROVAL. SHE WOULDN'T MEET HIS STARE.

SHE SECURED A **REAL** APARTMENT THAT DAY, AND WAS LEAVING THE HOUSE.

THE LITTLE FELLOW LEFT THE ROOM AS WE BATHED HER IN CONGRATULATIONS.

I WISHED I HAD DONE THAT TO THE CAT LOVER.

LATER SHE GRAVITATED TO ME AGAIN, AND ASKED IF I WANTED TO COME SEE HER APARTMENT. NO NEUROSIS AND AN ADMIRABLE DISPLAY OF TAKING POSITIVE DIRECTIONS WITH HER LIFE. I FELT EXCITED AND A BIT DRUNK.

SOMEONE OVERHEARD AND TOOK IT AS AN INVITATION TO CONTINUE THE ENTIRE PARTY AT HER APARTMENT. I DETECTED A LITTLE DISAPPOINTMENT IN HER, BUT SHE DIDN'T LET IT SPOIL HER CELEBRATION. SHE DOESN'T EVEN POUT! ANOTHER ADMIRABLE TRAIT.

SHE HADN'T MOVED IN YET; JUST A FEW BOXES, HER STEREO, AND ENOUGH WOOD TO CHRISTEN THE FIREPLACE.

7.

A FEW HOURS LATER, AND FEELING A BIT MORE DRUNK, I COULDN'T DECIDE IF I WANTED TO LEAVE. BUT OTHERS WERE DEPARTING IN TWOS AND THREES AND I ALSO DIDN'T WANT IT TO APPEAR THAT I PLANNED TO STAY.

IT ENDED UP BEING JUST ME AND ONE OTHER GUY, WHICH LOOKED INNOCENT ENOUGH...

BUT HE PASSED OUT SHORTLY AFTER, AND IT WAS AS THOUGH WE WERE ALONE.

SHE STARTED COMPLETELY SHARING HER LIFE WITH ME. SHOWING ME HIGH SCHOOL YEARBOOKS AND PHOTO ALBUMS.

SHE WENT FURTHER INTO HER BREAK-UP, AND SHOWED ME A BOOK SHE WAS READING. A SUPERMARKET SELF-HELP BOOK ON "CO-DEPENDENCY."

COUPLES PERPETUATING BAD RELATIONSHIPS OUT OF A NEED TO FEED OFF EACH OTHER'S PROBLEMS OR SOME SUCH RUBBISH. THERE'S THE NEUROSIS. I KNEW IT.

⑧.

BUT SHE SEEMS TO BE DOING SOMETHING ABOUT IT. CLEANING HOUSE WITH HER LIFE.

I FELT OUT OF CONTROL, AND SORT OF DETATCHED MYSELF. I FELT LIKE I WAS HOVERING OVER US, LISTENING TO OUR CONVERSATION.

I WAS GOING TO BE WISE AND CAUTIOUS.

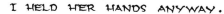

I HELD HER HANDS ANYWAY.

THE KNOCK AT THE DOOR KNOCKED HER HANDS RIGHT OUT OF MINE.

HER EXPRESSION OF FEAR TURNED TO DETER-MINATION. "IT'S **HIM**," SHE SAID.

"I TOLD HIM TO STAY THE HELL AWAY FROM HERE."

9.

I JUST SAT TO DRINK MY BEER WHILE SHE WENT AT IT.

SHE WALKED TALL AND PROUD UNTIL SHE OPENED THE DOOR.

WITH EVERY SENTENCE HE SPOKE, HER POSTURE SLUMPED, AND HER HEAD TIPPED DOWN.

I COULDN'T HEAR THE WORDS, BUT IT WAS LIKE LISTENING TO A SONG. THE TELLING MUSIC NOTES OF A CONVERSATION. THE UPS AND DOWNS AND REPEATING VERSES. YOU COULD TELL WHICH NOTES DOMINATED THE SONG, AND THEY WEREN'T HERS. I HAD TO SNEAK PAST THIS SAD TUNE AND GET OUT OF THERE.

SHE WOULDN'T EVEN LOOK AT ME.

ON THE WAY HOME I FELT LIKE KILLING A CAT. I DIDN'T.

10.

SHE APPARENTLY GAVE UP THE APARTMENT. THE NEXT DAY SHE WAS BACK AT THE HOUSE. BACK IN HIS ROOM.

SHE NEVER SPOKE OF IT TO ME, OR IGNORED ME EITHER, REALLY. WE JUST EXCHANGED THE USUAL ROOMMATE PLEASANTRIES.

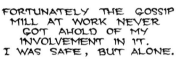
FORTUNATELY THE GOSSIP MILL AT WORK NEVER GOT AHOLD OF MY INVOLVEMENT IN IT. I WAS SAFE, BUT ALONE.

SHE WOULD BE SO LOVELY, IF NOT FOR THE NEUROSES AND INSECURITIES.

BUT THEN, I DON'T TRY TO CHANGE PEOPLE.

11.
End.

41

ESCAPE #2: The Dry Creek Bed

I HAD TO ESCAPE FARTHER THIS TIME, AND THE DRY CREEK BED WAS GOING TO BE MY RUNWAY.

FROM UP ON THE CITY STREETS, I WAS ALWAYS FASCINATED BY THE OLD WATERWAY, WISHING I COULD JUMP DOWN FROM THE PAVEMENT AND MAKE IT MY OWN PERSONAL HIGHWAY.

I'VE WISHED I COULD FOLLOW ITS ENDLESS WINDING UNTIL I DISAPPEARED.

THE DAY TO DO IT CAME.

IT WAS LATE SUMMER, AND THERE WAS ONLY A FEW ISOLATED POOLS OF WATER IN WHAT WAS ONCE A ROARING CHANNEL. IT WAS STRANGE TO HAVE SUCH AN ALIEN PLACE IN THE MIDDLE OF THE CITY.

©1992 Jeff Nicholson

THERE WAS ACTUALLY A SMALL AMOUNT OF WILDLIFE DOWN HERE. A MUSTY FROG-SMELL CAME FROM THE DRIED-OUT WASHED GRASS.

CAVE-LIKE EROSIONS FORMED UNDER TREE ROOTS, WHICH I'M SURE MUST HOUSE SOME SORT OF ANIMALS.

HUMANITY'S PRESENCE WAS STILL FAIRLY DOMINANT THOUGH. GARBAGE. SHOPPING CARTS.

SLABS AND IRON AND OTHER CITY DEBRIS. I NEEDED TO MOVE FURTHER ON.

THE FARTHER OUT OF TOWN I WENT, THE THICKER THE TREES BECAME, HIDING THE CITY LANDMARKS THAT PASSED BY.

SOMETHING STIRRED IN THE BRUSH AND I FOOLISHLY THOUGHT I WOULD GLIMPSE A POSSUM OR SKUNK OR RACCOON.

2.

A CAT RAN OUT. NOT JUST A CAT BUT A WILD CAT. THE WORST KIND.

THEY SEEM TO HATE HUMANS, AND ENJOY SHOWING OFF THAT YOU COULD NEVER CATCH THEM.

I HAD BEEN WALKING HALF THE DAY BUT STILL DIDN'T SEEM TO BE GETTING OUT OF TOWN. AN AREA THAT LOOKED WILD FROM A DISTANCE WOULD IN REALITY HAVE A MAZE OF TRAILS RUNNING THROUGH IT.

AN ELABORATE FREEWAY SYSTEM CREATED BY COMMUTING SCHOOL CHILDREN, CLASS-CUTTING TEENAGERS, AND HOMELESS DRIFTERS.

I DIDN'T KNOW WHERE I WAS GOING, OR WHEN I WOULD BE BACK, BUT I BROUGHT IN MY PACK A FLASHLIGHT, A BEDROLL, AND SOME MATCHES FOR A FIRE.

I CRAWLED OUT ONTO STREET LEVEL FOR A FINAL STOCKING OF FOODSTUFFS.

Vern's LIQUOR

I SOON CAME UPON A HOMELESS CAMP OF SOME SORT.

THEY SEEMED TO HAVE AN ELABORATE CULTURE BUILT UP AROUND THE SALVAGING OF RECYCLABLE ITEMS. FROM HERE THEY COULD VENTURE INTO THE CITY AND COLLECT CANS AND BOTTLES AND SCRAP METALS, AND SOMEHOW MAKE A LIVING FROM IT.

I COULD JOIN UP WITH THEM, BUT WHY WOULD FORAGING FOR TRASH FROM GUTTERS BE ANY DIFFERENT THAN FORAGING FOR MY SUPERIORS AT WORK?

THEY DIDN'T SEEM DANGEROUS, SO I PASSED ON BY. IN A SURREAL WAY, THEY SEEMED LIKE POST-APOCALYPTIC SURVIVORS. HUMAN MUTATIONS THAT ATE ALUMINUM AND PLASTIC INSTEAD OF FOOD.

I WALKED UNTIL TWILIGHT, AND FINALLY SEEMED TO BE BEYOND THE CITY. I PEEKED OUT OF THE CREEK BED, AND SAW ONLY A FEW SMALL ROADS AND FENCES. **I WAS ESCAPING!**

THEN JUST A FEW MINUTES LATER, I SAW A FIGURE APPROACHING FROM THE OPPOSITE WAY I CAME. HE STOPPED, PERHAPS UNSURE OF MY PRESENCE AHEAD OF HIM, THEN CONTINUED.

AT CLOSER RANGE, HE STOPPED AGAIN. I COULD TELL HE SAW ME. HIS POSTURE SEEMED TO SLUMP.

THEN HE WHEELED AROUND AND STARTED BACK THE OTHER WAY.

4.

I WASN'T SURE IF I SHOULD STOP OR CONTINUE ON. THIS PERSON MUST HAVE COME FROM SOMEWHERE. SOMEWHERE BEYOND THE CATS AND CRAZY GIRLS AND TIRED ILLUSTRATIONS.

I KEPT GOING, KEEPING JUST FAR ENOUGH BEHIND TO KEEP HIM IN SIGHT. THERE WAS ENOUGH OF A MOON THAT I DIDN'T NEED MY FLASHLIGHT.

WE WALKED FOR PERHAPS TWO HOURS. IF HE WASN'T GOING TO SPEND THE NIGHT OUT HERE, HE MUST BE PLANNING ON REACHING SOMEWHERE TONIGHT... BUT WHERE?

I LOST TRACK OF TIME, STUMBLING OVER THE UNCHANGING SMOOTH STONES AND SKINNY WEEDS.

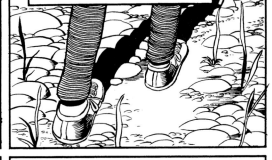

THEN I THOUGHT I SAW A WALL AHEAD, WHICH MADE NO SENSE. WHAT WOULD A WALL BE DOING OUT IN THE MIDDLE OF THE COUNTRY? BUT IT WAS REAL, AND IT HAD A BLACK OPENING IN IT.

IT LOOKED LIKE A CARTOON WALL WITH A PAINTED DOOR. LIKE I WOULD CRASH INTO IT AFTER WATCHING HIM PASS THROUGH.

THE DOOR WAS REAL, TOO; THE PITCHEST OF BLACK INSIDE. IT WAS A TUNNEL THAT SEEMED TO GO ON FOREVER.

I NEEDED MY FLASHLIGHT TO GET PAST THE INDISTINCT DEBRIS ALONG THE WAY. THERE WAS A LIGHT AT THE OTHER END, BUT I COULDN'T FOR THE LIFE OF ME FIGURE OUT WHERE IT WOULD LEAD.

MAYBE I HAD SPREAD OUT MY BEDROLL HOURS AGO, AND I WAS DREAMING ALL OF THIS. OR THIS WAS SOME ASTRAL MESSENGER, COME TO GRANT ME MY ESCAPE

THE DOOR TO HEAVEN OR HELL WAS GETTING CLOSER, THE MESSENGER ALREADY BEYOND IT.

THIS IS MY REWARD FOR BELIEVING THERE IS SOMETHING OTHER THAN WHAT I KNOW BACK THERE. THIS IS...

THIS IS ANOTHER CITY. JUST LIKE MINE.

THIS MESSENGER IS JUST ANOTHER ME, ESCAPING.

I YELLED OBSCENITIES AT HIM AND TURNED BACK.

6.
End.

"BE CREATIVE"

©1992 Jeff Nicholson
Lettering: Chad Woody

THERE IS A MAN, OR A WOMAN, WHO TAPS THE SIDE OF MY HEAD, AND I CAN NEVER SEE WHO IT IS.

THE TAP WOULD PUNCTURE MY TEMPLE WITHOUT WARNING.

I WOULD INSTANTLY FEEL A LITHIUM-LIKE EUPHORIA, AND IN THE TIME IT WOULD TAKE TO TURN MY HEAD AROUND, THEY WOULD BE GONE.

THE MANAGEMENT AND SALES PEOPLE TAP ME WITH NO SECRECY. IT IS MY JOB TO ACCEPT IT.

THE ONE WHO WANTS MY TEMPLE DOES NOT EVEN GRANT ME THE COURTESY OF A FACE-TO-FACE PLUNDERING OF MY JUICE.

SOMEDAY I WILL LEARN WHO THIS PERSON IS.

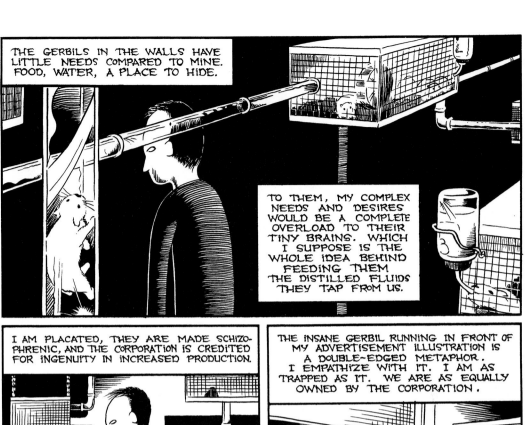

THE GERBILS IN THE WALLS HAVE LITTLE NEEDS COMPARED TO MINE. FOOD, WATER, A PLACE TO HIDE.

TO THEM, MY COMPLEX NEEDS AND DESIRES WOULD BE A COMPLETE OVERLOAD TO THEIR TINY BRAINS. WHICH I SUPPOSE IS THE WHOLE IDEA BEHIND FEEDING THEM THE DISTILLED FLUIDS THEY TAP FROM US.

I AM PLACATED, THEY ARE MADE SCHIZO- PHRENIC, AND THE CORPORATION IS CREDITED FOR INGENUITY IN INCREASED PRODUCTION.

THE INSANE GERBIL RUNNING IN FRONT OF MY ADVERTISEMENT ILLUSTRATION IS A DOUBLE-EDGED METAPHOR. I EMPATHIZE WITH IT. I AM AS TRAPPED AS IT. WE ARE AS EQUALLY OWNED BY THE CORPORATION.

BUT I AM ALSO SUPERIOR TO IT. IT IS MORTIFIED AND MUST RUN.

I CAN SIT AND PRODUCE AND FOCUS MYSELF AND BE REWARDED FOR DOING SO.

I HAVE BEEN DRAINED OF THE FLUIDS THAT MAKE IT CRAZY.

2.

AND IF I FEEL THE NEED...

I CAN KILL IT. I CAN MAKE THE PAIN STOP.

AT LEAST THAT'S WHAT THEY TELL ME. I SOUND LIKE A COMPANY MAN, QUOTING THE COMPANY PHILOSOPHY. BUT IT'S ALL FALSE.

EVEN ON FRIDAY, WHEN EVERYONE IS HAPPY, I FEEL LITTLE DIFFERENCE.

WE'VE BEEN TRICKED INTO BEING HYPED UP FOR A "GREAT WEEKEND." BUT WHY ARE FIVE DAYS THEIRS, TWO OURS?

THE OTHERS BEHAVE AS THOUGH IT IS A NATURAL CONDITION. ALL OF THE DAYS SHOULD BE MINE.

AND THE WORST IS THAT I MUST "BE CREATIVE." THERE IS EVEN A BOX MARKED "BE CREATIVE" ON THE ILLUSTRATION REQUISITION SLIPS, AS THOUGH IT IS A TOGGLE SWITCH IN MY HEAD.

Illustration Request
Client _RICO'S PIZZA_
Sales Rep _KELLI_
N&R _X_ G.W. _____ Other _____
☐ Rush ☒ Be Creative

3.

I AM NEEDED TO THINK OF THINGS OTHERS ARE INCAPABLE OF, WHILE THOSE SAME PEOPLE ARE DRAINING THE JUICES NECESSARY TO DO IT.

WHAT COMES OUT ISN'T CREATIVE. IT IS JUST FLATLY ACHIEVED, SHOVELLED OUT BY ATROPHIED MUSCLES, BUT THEY DON'T SEEM TO NOTICE THE DIFFERENCE.

SO MY DREAMS, THAT SCURRY AWAY THROUGH HABITRAIL TUBES, MUST BE WAYLAYED WHILE I FULFILL THE LIMITED DREAMS OF SALES REPRESENTATIVES.

BUT IT IS NOW THE "GREAT WEEKEND." LIKE A SCHIZOPHRENIC GERBIL, I RACE TO MY PLACE TO HIDE, AND TRY TO SUCKLE NOURISHMENT FROM THE JUICES I NEED.

BUT I AM SO DRIED INSIDE I WANT IT ALL IMMEDIATELY. I CAN'T PERCEIVE THAT THERE WILL BE HUNDREDS OF WEEKENDS AND AN ENTIRE LIFE AHEAD OF ME.

I COULD BE SMASHED LIKE THE THROWAWAY GERBIL AT ANY MOMENT. A WEEKEND WILL NEVER BE ENOUGH.

④

I WANT ALL MY BOOZE AND ALL MY FOOD AND ALL MY SEX AND ALL MY MUSIC ALL MY HOBBIES ALL MY TV MY PROJECTS MY PAINTINGS MY BAND MY ESCAPE JOURNEYS ALL NOW ALL THIS YEAR THIS SUMMER BEFORE IT GETS AWAY ALL THIS WEEKEND RIGHT NOW.

I HAVE CONVERTED MY HOBBIES AND ADDICTIONS INTO A SERIES OF HOSES TO FACILITATE THIS.

MY STIMULI IS TAKEN DIRECTLY TO MY NERVE ENDINGS AND ORIFICES AND I TAKE IT IN AND IN AND IN WITH CLENCHED TEETH AND A FIBRILATING HEARTBEAT.

5.

52

WITH SO MUCH INTAKE, THERE WAS LITTLE TIME FOR MY OWN CREATING. THE WEEKEND ENDED, AND I HAD TO TAKE MY 'RECHARGE BACK TO "BE CREATIVE" FOR THE TAPPERS.

I HAD AN IDEA OF WHO WAS DOING MY TEMPLE, TOO, AND I FINALLY THOUGHT OF A WAY TO SEE IT COMING.

I TOOK A PICTURE FRAME TO WORK, EMPTY EXCEPT FOR A BLACK MATTE BOARD AND PANE OF GLASS.

I HUNG IT IN FRONT OF ME AND TOLD EVERYONE IT WAS MY DREAM. MY EMPTY DREAM I WOULD SOME DAY FILL.

I SUPPOSE IT **WAS** THAT, BUT IT WAS ALSO NEARLY AS REFLECTIVE AS A MIRROR. I COULD SEE ANYONE APPROACHING ME NOW.

SUCH AS SALES REPS, SO LOST IN THEIR WORLD OF GLAD~HANDING, THEY WILL BLINDLY SLAP THE BACK OF SOMEONE IN THE MIDDLE OF A DRAFTED LINE OF INK.

THE SALESPERSON'S REFLECTION WAS REPLACED BY ANOTHER.

A FIGURE THAT WAS VAGUELY FAMILIAR, BUT ONE WHICH I COULD NOT PLACE. IT STOPPED AND AN ARM CAME UP.

6.

I WHEELED AROUND BEFORE IT WAS TOO LATE. I BEAT HIM!	I LOOKED FLUSTERED, BUT THE MAN JUST LOWERED HIS EXTENDED ARM CALMLY, WITH NO INDICATION OF GUILT OR REMORSE.

"HOW ARE YOU, LAD?" HE ASKED. "FINE, SIR," MY RESPONSE.	"HOLD STILL FOR A MINUTE." "YES, SIR."

THIS MAN WAS NOT AFRAID TO CONFRONT ME. THIS MAN WAS THE OWNER OF THE CORPORATION. THIS MAN WAS TOO **BUSY** TO EVER HAVE SPOKEN TO ME.	I WAS TAPPED, AND WOULD RELAX. MY EMPTY DREAM WOULD WAIT.

ALL THESE TIRED DRAWINGS I DRAW TO SELL SOAP ARE ALL A PART OF THE GIANT DREAMS OF THIS MAN.	HE LIVES THE BENEFIT OF ALL THAT I DO, AND ALL THAT I DON'T.

7.
End.

ANIMAL CONTROL

THE NEIGHBORHOOD I LIVED IN WAS AN OLDER ONE.

EACH BLOCK HAD A DIRT OR GRAVEL ROAD RUNNING THROUGH THE MIDDLE OF IT.

I THINK THEY ORIGINALLY SERVED AS AN ACCESS TO EACH HOUSE'S GARAGE. THESE OLD LOTS WERE LONG AND NARROW, WITH A HOUSE IN THE FRONT, YARD IN THE MIDDLE, AND GARAGE IN THE BACK.

BUT WITH ALL THE OLD GARAGES HAVING BEEN EITHER TORN DOWN OR CONVERTED INTO RENTALS, THE ALLEYS NOW RAN THROUGH A PATCHWORK OF FENCES, TRASH CANS, AND ABANDONED CARS.

IT SEEMED DANGEROUS TO WANDER THROUGH THEM, BUT I LIKED THE FEELING. I LIKED THE SERENITY. THE IMAGES FOUND IN THIS STRANGE, DISORGANIZED, BACKSIDE OF HUMANITY.

UNTIL THE DOGS BARKED.

WITHOUT WARNING YOU'D BE FIVE FEET AWAY FROM SNARLING ANIMAL HATRED.

WHO OWNED THESE BEASTS? DID THEY ACTUALLY LIKE THEM? ARE THEY JUST THERE FOR PROTECTION?

WAS IT WORTH LISTENING TO THAT SAVAGE BARKING ALL THEIR LIVES JUST TO AVOID HAVING THEIR STEREO STOLEN?

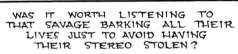

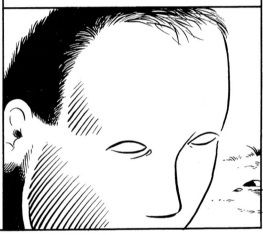

AND THE CATS. THE STRAYS BRED IN THESE PLACES.

EVEN IF YOU LIKED CATS, YOU COULDN'T WARM UP TO THESE MANGY, SCURRYING, RAT~LIKE PESTS.

2.

THEY REALLY MADE ME WONDER ABOUT THE DOMESTICATION OF ANIMALS.
I SUPPOSE ANCIENT MAN HAD SOME USE FOR DOGS.
GOD KNOWS WHY CATS WERE TAKEN INTO OUR HOMES.

ALONG THE MAIN STREETS IT WAS A DIFFERENT SCENE. FAT, CONTENT CATS SITTING ON FRONT PORCHES. PAMPERED POODLES TROTTING ACROSS LAWNS.

BUT BACK INTO THE ALLEYS WAS THE REALITY OF PETS. NO PEOPLE, JUST A GHETTO OF MISPLACED WILDLIFE.

THEY IRRITATED ME. THEY IRRITATED MY WALKS.

WHICH BRINGS ME TO THE POINT WHERE I FOUND THE GUN.

I COULDN'T BELIEVE IT WHEN I FIRST SAW IT. JUST LAYING THERE RIGHT IN THE OPEN.

IT MUST HAVE BEEN THROWN OVER A FENCE BY SOME PANICKED CREEP FLEEING THE POLICE, RECENTLY ENOUGH THAT NO ONE HAS SINCE WALKED BY TO FIND IT.

I SCOOPED IT UP AND HURRIED HOME.

I NEVER CARED MUCH FOR GUNS. NEVER REALLY HANDLED ONE. BUT IT WAS EXCITING TO HAVE MY OWN.

IT WAS A .22 I THINK. IT HELD NINE BULLETS. FOUR WERE FIRED AND FIVE WERE LEFT. I WANTED TO TRY IT.

57

I CUT A SLIT IN ONE OF MY JACKETS TO HIDE IT.

I PRACTISED HOW QUICKLY I COULD REMOVE IT WHILE CROUCHING, AIM, AND RETURN IT TO THE SLOT. I REPEATED IT OVER AND OVER UNTIL I COULD PERFORM THE MANEUVER IN ABOUT TWO SECONDS.

I PUT SOME BOOKS IN MY OLD COLLEGE BACKPACK. I WAS READY FOR A WALK IN THE ALLEYS AGAIN.

OF COURSE, NOW THAT I'M PREPARED, I COVER TWO BLOCKS WITHOUT SEEING ANY "PETS."

THEN A CAT POPS OUT OF A DUMPSTER LIKE AN ARCADE TARGET.

IT EVALUATES ME. A STRAY WILL GENERALLY PERCH AND STARE AT YOU FOR ABOUT THREE SECONDS BEFORE BOLTING.

I HAVE TWO.

NO ONE WILL THINK ANYTHING OF THE QUICK BANG. A CAR BACKFIRING. A NOISE. IT COULD BE ANYTHING.

EVEN IF SOMEONE LOOKED OUT A WINDOW TO INVEST- IGATE, I JUST LOOK LIKE A STUDENT.

EVEN THE MORE OBVIOUS SOUND OF TWO SHOTS...

ONE.

TWO.

...COULD BE PASSED OFF AS SOME DRUG DEAL CONFLICT NO ONE WANTS TO GET INVOLVED IN.

I GO A FEW MORE BLOCKS. DON'T WANT TO OVER DO IT.

5.

EVEN IF SOMEONE WAS POSITIVE
IT WAS THE SOUND OF A GUNSHOT...

BANG.

WOULD THEY COME
RUNNING OUT AND
CONFRONT A
STRANGER WITH,
"I THOUGHT I
HEARD GUNFIRE"?

I GO A FEW MORE BLOCKS.
ONLY ONE BULLET LEFT.

IT FEELS WEIRD. THIS MUST
BE HOW A SERIAL KILLER
FEELS. EXCEPT THESE ARE
JUST UNWANTED ANIMALS.

I GO ANOTHER
BLOCK WITH
NO TARGETS.
I START
FEELING
IMPATIENT.

I SCAN ALONG
THE BASES
OF THE
FENCES AS
I WALK,
LOOKING FOR
SCURRYING
CATS.

I SEE A PAIR
OF SHOES
WITH LEGS
IN THEM.

I LOOK UP AND IT'S A MAN.

HE DOESN'T SAY ANYTHING.
HE JUST STARES.

60

I STOP IN MY TRACKS WITHOUT THINKING.

HE ASSUMES A DOMINANT POSTURE. HE'S ONE OF THOSE ARROGANT ANIMAL TYPES THAT MAKE WOMEN HATE MEN. THAT MAKE **ME** HATE MEN.

HIS STARE IS A CHALLENGE.

AS THOUGH HE IS ALLOWED TO STARE, BUT IF I STARE BACK I'M CONSIDERED ASKING FOR TROUBLE.

I HAVE ONE BULLET LEFT. I COULD DROP HIM.

I TURN AND HEAD FOR HOME.

I BURY MY GUN WITH ITS ONE BULLET DEEP IN THE CLOSET.

I'M THINKING STRAIGHT. I THINK.

THAT WAS BEFORE THE GERBIL KING STARTED TELLING ME WHAT TO DO.

7.
End

61

WE NEVER REALLY UNDERSTOOD THE MAN WE CALLED THE INFILTRATOR.

THE INFILTRATOR

WE ALL WENT TO THE SAME DESIGN SCHOOL, EXCEPT FOR HIM.

WE ALL SERVED AN INTERNSHIP HERE DURING OUR LAST YEAR OF COLLEGE.

WE ALL CAME TO WORK FOR THIS COMPANY OUT OF DESPAIR AFTER GRADUATION.

EXCEPT FOR HIM. HE **WANTED** TO BE HERE. HE WORKED HIS WAY UP, WITH NO EXPERIENCE, AND NEVER SAID A NEGATIVE WORD ABOUT THE CORPORATION.

HE WAS ONCE QUOTED AS SAYING, "WE SHOULD BE PAYING **THEM** TO LET US WORK HERE."

MANY WILD THEORIES GREW UP AROUND HIS ORIGINS. THAT HE WAS A SPY, SENT BY ANOTHER COMPANY TO GAIN TRADE SECRETS. OR FROM OUR OWN CORPORATE HEADQUARTERS, TO WATCH PRODUCTIVITY FIRST HAND. OR EVEN A GOVERNMENT MAN, PLANTED TO UNCOVER SOME SINISTER CONSPIRACY OF OURS.

THE REASON FOR OUR SUSPICIONS WAS THE WAY HE DEVOURED INFORMATION. HE ALWAYS SEEMED TO BE TAKING NOTES, BUT DENIED DOING SO. SOMEONE EVEN SWORE HE CONCEALED A MINIATURE CAMERA.

THESE FACTS WERE UNSUBSTANTIATED, BUT I COULD FEEL THE DIFFERENCE BETWEEN HIS INQUISITIVENESS AND THAT OF HIS GOSSIP PARTNER, THE BLONDE ONE.

WHEN SHE WOULD PRY, SHE WOULD ONLY HALF LISTEN TO YOUR ANSWER, SCANNING FOR TIDBITS ON ROMANCE OR SCANDAL.

IF NONE WERE FORTHCOMING, SHE WOULD STOP LISTENING ENTIRELY.

THE INFILTRATOR WANTED **ALL** INFORMATION ANYONE HAD TO OFFER. TO THE POINT OF IRRITATION.

TAPPED COMPLETELY DRY FROM THE MISERABLE ILLUSTRATIONS I HAD TO PRODUCE, THE INFILTRATOR WOULD DRAIN ME FURTHER WITH HIS INCESSANT IN~ TEREST IN WHATEVER I WAS DRAWING.

HE WOULD COERCE ME INTO TELLING THE STORY BEHIND IT, BUT I DIDN'T LIKE TO BERATE MY OWN DRAWINGS, (FOR MY OWN EGO'S SAKE, AND TO AVOID BECOMING LIKE THE DOOMED ONE WHO WORKED BESIDE ME).

SO NOT ONLY WOULD I HAVE TO CREATE USELESS, PROSTITUTIONAL ARTWORK, I WOULD HAVE TO VERBALLY PRETEND IT WAS INTERESTING.

WHICH IS WHY, SELFISH AS IT WAS, I WAS GLAD TO HEAR HE WAS KILLED IN AN AUTOMOBILE ACCIDENT.

2

63

IT DID NOT SEEM TO BE A GREAT LOSS TO ANYONE ELSE, EITHER. NO ONE WAS REALLY CLOSE, OR SEEMED TO MISS HIM.

DESPITE HIS MANIC INQUISITIVENESS, HE WAS A VERY FORGETTABLE PERSON. HIS INTERESTS AND TASTES WERE AS MAINSTREAM AND IMPASSIONATE AS POSSIBLE.

JUST AN AVERAGE PERSON THAT DIED IN AN AVERAGE CAR IN AN AVERAGE ACCIDENT ON AN AVERAGE STREET.

UNTIL THE GOVERNMENT MAN CAME TO OUR COMMUNAL HOME.

WE THOUGHT OUR OLD SUSPICIONS MUST BE TRUE. PERHAPS THEY JUST UNCOVERED A LOST REPORT BY THE INFILTRATOR, AND WERE COMING AFTER ONE OF US.

IT WAS ONLY A MATTER OF HIS ESTATE. THE GOVERNMENT SEIZED HIS FINANCES, COULD FIND NO IMMEDIATE FAMILY, AND HANDED HIS KEYS, AT RANDOM, TO **ME**.

IT WAS IRONIC WE WERE BEING GIVEN HIS POSSESSIONS, SINCE WE HAD ALREADY LOOTED HIS ROOM OF ANY CD's, CLOTHING, OR SPARE CHANGE.

3

BUT THE KEY WENT TO THE CLOSET, WHICH NONE OF US PETTY THIEVES WAS BRASH ENOUGH TO HAVE FORCED OPEN.

WE ALL KNEW THE INFILTRATOR'S OLD ROOM HAD AN ENORMOUS WALK-IN CLOSET. NOW IT WAS AS THOUGH GOD AND THE GOVERNMENT HAD GIVEN US PERMISSION TO INVADE IT.

WE KNEW THIS WAS WHAT ALL THE NOTES AND SECRET PICTURES WERE ABOUT.

THE CLOSET WAS LINED WITH SHELVES, ALL FILLED WITH FOLDERS AND BINDERS AND VIDEO TAPES, THREE ROWS DEEP. HOW WAS IT THAT HIS SUPERIORS, WHOEVER THEY WERE, DIDN'T GET THEIR HANDS ON THIS BEFORE US?

4

WE ALL GRABBED SOMETHING AND STARTED THUMBING THROUGH IT.
IT FELT SLIGHTLY DANGEROUS. ONCE WE TAMPERED AND LEARNED,
THERE WOULD BE NO TURNING BACK FROM OUR INVOLVEMENT.

I WAS SHOCKED AT THE TITLE OF THE VOLUME I HELD. IT BORE THE NAME OF ONE OF MY WORKMATES, THE DATES JANUARY 18th THROUGH NOVEMBER 6th OF THIS YEAR, AND THE WORD "LUNCHES."

INSIDE WERE PHOTOS OF PLATES OF FOOD, WITH DATES AND A RESTAURANT NAME UNDER THEM.

I SHOWED THEM TO THE MAN WHOSE FOOD STARRED IN THIS BINDER, AND WITH HIS MEMORY JOGGED, THESE WERE INDEED THE LUNCHES HE ATE WITH THE INFILTRATOR DURING THOSE MONTHS.

WE COULD NOT IMAGINE WHAT PROJECT COULD REQUIRE SUCH INTENSE DOCUMENTATION.

THE OTHER FILES PROVED EVEN MORE BIZARRE. LISTS OF WHICH EMPLOYEES LIKED WHICH KINDS OF MUSIC. WHO HAD DATED WHO AND WHEN.

SECRET PHOTOS CAPTURING THE DAYS WHEN SOMEONE HAD A CHANGE IN HAIRSTYLE.

MUSIC CROSS-REFERENCE

NONE OF IT SEEMED LIKE COMPELLING INFORMATION... JUST RANDOM TRIVIA.

Temp below 78° - she chooses hot chocolate (over 90% of time).

Temp above 78 she chooses diet Coke (doesn't recycle cans).

PORING THROUGH THE REAMS OF JOURNAL NOTES, I LEARNED THAT THERE WAS NO "BOSS" BEHIND THIS. THE INFILTRATOR WAS OBSESSED BY DOCUMENTATION, AND FASCINATED WITH THE LIVES OF THOSE AROUND HIM.

HIS LIFE, ITSELF, WAS NOTHING. NO DREAMS OR VISIONS. NO REAL HOBBIES OR CREATIVE PROCESSES. JUST A MASSIVE FETISH WITH OUR LIVES.

WE FELT USED, EMBARRASSED, AND SOMEHOW UNWORTHY.

THE INFILTRATOR CREATED AN UNWANTED DOCUMENTARY. A MASSIVE TESTAMENT TO HIS LIFE, WHICH WOULD JUST AS QUICKLY BE FORGOTTEN.

6
End

ESCAPE #3: Concow

I HAVE TRIED TO ESCAPE INTO PLACES UNKNOWN, AND HAVE FAILED.

LOOKING FOR MYSTERY AND ADVENTURE, I HAVE FOUND THE SAME CORRUPTION AND DECAY THAT MY WORKPLACE IS BUILT UPON.

I DECIDED TO GO SOME-WHERE I ALWAYS WENT AS A BOY. I TOOK MAPS AND MEMORIES AND I WOULD FIND IT.

IT WAS FAR INTO THE MOUNTAINS ON DIRT ROADS, BUT I HAD MY WELFARE WAGON.

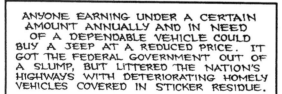

THAT'S SLANG FOR THE GOVERNMENT POSTAL JEEP I BOUGHT. AFTER THE MAIL SYSTEM WENT BANKRUPT AND PRIVATE ENTERPRISE TOOK IT OVER, THE JEEPS WERE USED IN A GENERAL ASSISTANCE PROGRAM.

ANYONE EARNING UNDER A CERTAIN AMOUNT ANNUALLY AND IN NEED OF A DEPENDABLE VEHICLE COULD BUY A JEEP AT A REDUCED PRICE. IT GOT THE FEDERAL GOVERNMENT OUT OF A SLUMP, BUT LITTERED THE NATION'S HIGHWAYS WITH DETERIORATING HOMELY VEHICLES COVERED IN STICKER RESIDUE.

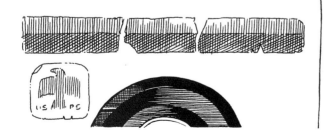

OVERNIGHT MAIL
PM 4MT
$10.45

1

BUT I DIDN'T CARE ABOUT THAT. I WAS GOING TO CONCOW. I HAD FOUND THE TURN OFF.

CONCOW WAS A TINY VALLEY COMMUNITY. I HAD NO IDEA OF THE POPULATION. MOSTLY VACATION CABINS AND TRAILERS HIDDEN IN THE FOLIAGE.

SEVERAL MILES IN WAS HOFFMAN ROAD, ENTRANCE TO A NETWORK OF DIRT ROADS. MY COUSINS AND I KNEW EVERY INCH OF THEM.

I DREW MAPS OF THEM WITH FELT PENS WHILE MY PARENTS COOKED HAMBURGERS ON THE CAMPFIRE.

I WAS SURPRISED TO SEE IT PAVED NOW.

IT WAS A BACK-TO-NATURE KICK OR SOMETHING FOR MY PARENTS' GENERATION. NO ONE LIVED UP THERE FULL-TIME, BUT WE KNEW WHO OWNED ALL THE PARCELS OF LAND.

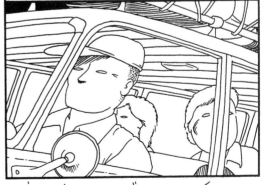

MY MAP PROVED THIS FRONTIERS-MAN-LIKE KNOW-LEDGE.

VIELBIGS · ADDAMS · DIVINES · HUBBARDS · OLD LAKE RD. · SAUNDERS · DIAMOND NATIONAL · LOGGING ROADS · CONCOW RD. · SMOKE ROAD · WARDS · HULLY GULLY · HOFFMAN ROAD · FERN PATCH · KENTS · US! · "HOG RANCH"

2.

THE VEILBIGS. SOMETIMES THEY WOULD
BE UP ON THE SAME WEEKEND.

I WAS SURPRISED TO SEE THEIR
OLD PLACE DESERTED.

HALF-WAY UP HOFFMAN ROAD THE PAVE-
MENT RETURNED TO DIRT.
I WAS RELIEVED PROGRESS HADN'T
CLAIMED ALL OF IT.

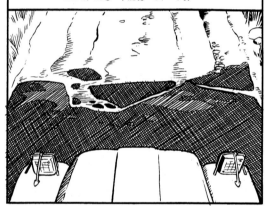

NEXT ON MY MAP WAS **SMOKE ROAD**.
A SECRET ROAD FOR US.

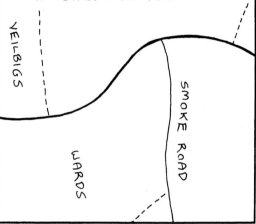

WE SWIPED SOME CIGARETTES FROM MY
PARENTS AND WENT THERE TO PRETEND
WE WERE COWBOY "MARLBORO MEN."

IT DIDN'T LOOK LIKE SOMEWHERE
I WANTED TO GO NOW.

HULLY GULLY.
A GOOD PLACE TO CATCH LIZARDS.

I WAS SURPRISED TO SEE PEOPLE LIVING THERE. I GUESS SOME WELFARE TYPES HAD MOVED IN OVER THE YEARS.

OUR OLD PARCEL WAS AT THE END. I WAS SURE THINGS WERE BETTER BACK THERE.

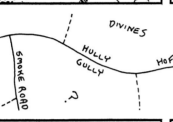

DIVINES

HULLY GULLY

SMOKE ROAD

HOFFMAN ROAD

'' RD.

JUNDERS

FERN PATCH

KENTS

US!

?

THE FERN PATCH. ONE OF THE FEW OPEN GLADES IN THE AREA.

I DON'T THINK SURPRISED WAS THE RIGHT WORD ANYMORE. I DIDN'T UNDERSTAND WHAT I WAS SEEING AT FIRST. TO THE RIGHT WAS ALL FENCED UP.

THERE WERE ALL THESE CHICKENS WALKING AROUND. BIG BLACK ROOSTERS WITH COLORED PLUMES. EACH MEAN~ LOOKING BIRD HAD ITS OWN PRIVATE COOP MADE OF A STEEL OIL DRUM.

DO THEY STILL HAVE COCK FIGHTS IN THIS COUNTRY?
I DIDN'T WANT TO STOP AND ASK.

I APPROACHED OUR OLD PARCEL. I REMEMBER THE BOTTOM OF THE HILL WHERE WE DUG THE WELL.

IT SEEMED THAT EVERYONE DECIDED TO MAKE THIS END OF THE LINE LOT THE LOCAL DUMP NOW.

BEYOND THAT WAS DIAMOND NATIONAL FOREST. A LOGGING RESERVE. THE REAL FRONTIER. THE ROAD WAS ROUGH, BUT MY JEEP COULD HANDLE IT.

I PASSED A VAN AND SOME CRAZY MAN STAMMERED AT ME, "DON'T GO RIGHT, DON'T GO RIGHT."

HE LAUGHED A TOOTHLESS GRIN AND TRIED TO DRIVE AWAY IN NEUTRAL, PROBABLY DRUNK. I HAD TO RAM THE BUSHES TO GET PAST.

FIRST I WOULD FIND THE "HOG RANCH." A SETTLEMENT FROM THE 1800's WE USED TO EXPLORE AS KIDS.

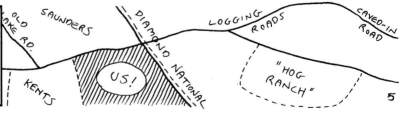

5

THEY MISTOOK MY JEEP FOR A FEDERAL INVESTIGATOR'S. THEY SEARCHED IT AND MYSELF, NEITHER OF WHICH CARRIED ANYTHING OF VALUE.

THEY ASKED IF I KNEW OF ANYONE WHO WANTED TO BUY FOOD STAMPS AT "70 ON THE DOLLAR." I WAS LUCKY TO GET AWAY WITH MY LIFE.

I CONTINUED MY ODYSSEY IN SPITE OF THEM. I HAD TO GET TO THE "BURNT FOREST." A PLACE WHERE A LIGHTNING FIRE CONSUMED AN ENTIRE RANGE. I LOVED THE SURREAL POST-NUCLEAR EFFECT.

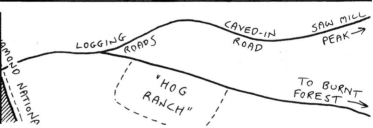

MONO NATIONA

LOGGING ROADS

CAVED-IN ROAD

SAW MILL PEAK →

"HOG RANCH"

TO BURNT FOREST →

I WAS DESCENDING A HILL WHEN I REALIZED SOMETHING WAS BESIDE THE ROAD.

A HORSE. A HORRIBLE DEAD HORSE. BEFORE I COULD TAKE IN WHAT I WAS SEEING, THE SMELL HIT ME.

6

I HAD NEVER SMELLED UNBREATHABLE AIR BEFORE. I HAD TO COVER MY FACE.

I COULD SEE A MAGGOT~SWARM IN IT'S EYE SOCKET AND THE HILL WAS TOO STEEP TO BACK UP AND I COULD ONLY DRIVE WITH ONE HAND.

I JUST GASSED IT DOWN THE HILL, TRYING TO SHAKE THE THOUGHT OF A GALLOPING GHOST HORSE OFF MY TAIL.

I STOPPED A GOOD QUARTER~MILE AWAY. JEEZUS, IT WAS JUST A DUMB HORSE. I FELT LIKE IT WAS GOING TO GET ME. IT JUST WASN'T RIGHT, IT BEING THERE. IT MADE EVERYTHING SEEM WRONG.

I HAD TO GO HOME. I HAD TO GET PAST THAT STUPID HORSE AND GET HOME. IT WASN'T KILLED AS A LAME. ONE SHOT TO THE HEAD WOULD'VE BEEN THE WAY TO DO THAT.

IT TOOK A SHOTGUN BLAST TO THE SIDE THAT LEFT A MAGGOT~SWARM THE SIZE OF A LARGE PIZZA.

I CAN'T GO BACK TO THE PAST. I CAN'T ESCAPE INTO THE FUTURE. I CAN'T ESCAPE INTO THE PRESENT.

THE GERBIL KING CRAWLS OUT OF MY SHIRT AND TELLS ME...
...IT TOLD ME SO.

7 End.

DARK SPIRAL

MY CO-WORKER WHO HAD SERVED AS A SURROGATE GERBIL FOR THE CORPORATION SUDDENLY ASKED, AFTER SIX MONTHS IN A WIRE CAGE, TO BE RETURNED TO HIS POST AS COPYWRITER. I MISSED HIM. HE WAS MY FAVORITE WORKMATE. MAYBE NOW THINGS WOULD BE BETTER. WE COULD JOKE AROUND LIKE WE USED TO. I COULD PULL MYSELF OUT OF THIS DOWNHILL SLIDE.

I ASKED HIM IF HE REMEMBERED WHAT IT WAS LIKE IN THE CAGE, IF HE HAD BEEN AWARE OF HIS SURROUNDINGS. "OF COURSE," HE ANSWERED. THEN WHISPERED, "THAT'S WHEN I WROTE MY BOOK."

DARK SPIRAL WAS THE TITLE. BUT IT WAS ONLY ONE PAGE LONG. SO HE WROTE A BOOK CALLED ABOUT DARK SPIRAL. ONE WAS THE STORY. ONE WAS ABOUT WRITING THE STORY.

WRITING THE STORY IN YOUR HEAD FOR SIX MONTHS WHILE IN A WIRE GERBIL CAGE. BEING IN A WIRE GERBIL CAGE FOR SIX MONTHS BECAUSE OF TAKING L.S.D. CONSTANTLY THE SIX MONTHS PRIOR TO THAT.

HE LET ME READ IT.
IT WAS GOOD.
IT WAS GREAT.

THE ONE-PAGER SUMMED UP, IN A VERY MOVING WAY, THAT YOU DON'T LEARN ANYTHING FROM DRUGS. THAT LIFE IS A DARK SPIRAL. THAT A WOULD-BE WRITER WHO NEVER ACTUALLY WRITES IS ONLY A PROCRASTINATING SHAM.

ABOUT DARK SPIRAL OPENS WITH A BELIEF THAT DRUGS ARE A PATHWAY TO DISCOVERING SOMETHING. ALL MY WORKMATE DISCOVERED WAS THAT AFTER TRYING TO BE A WRITER FOR A YEAR ALL HE COULD COME UP WITH WAS ONE PAGE.

BUT THE IRONY OF IT WAS THAT IN TELLING THE TALE OF GETTING TO THAT ONE PAGE, HE HAD PRODUCED AN INTRIGUING SHORT NOVEL.

HIS WRITING PARALLELED MY DRAWING. HE DESPISED WRITING INSIPID COPY FOR THE CORPORATION AS MUCH AS I DESPISED ILLUSTRATING SMILING CONSUMERS. WE FOUND SOLACE IN EACH OTHER, HYPING OURSELVES UP FOR THE IDEA, NO, THE **FACT** THAT WE WOULD LEAVE THIS COMPANY FAR BEHIND WITHIN A YEAR.

2.

THIS TALK MADE THE OTHERS UNCOMFORTABLE. IT SUGGESTED WE HAD A POWER THEY LACKED. A POWER TO ESCAPE.

BUT HOW COULD WE FOCUS THIS POWER? THE ANSWER TO THAT CAME, STRIKINGLY, FROM ONE OF THE VERY CLIENTS THE CORP- ORATION DRAINED OUR JUICES TO PLEASE.

HE WAS A SNAKE~OIL MAN, BUT HE HAD MONEY. I DIDN'T EVEN REMEMBER WHAT WORK WE DID FOR HIM, BUT HE WANTED TO MEET THE BOTH OF US.

HE WANTED TO TALK AFTER HOURS IN ONE OF HIS "CLUBS", LIKE IT WAS SOME HIGH FINANCE CONSPIRACY. WE WERE MILDLY CURIOUS, SUSPICIOUS OF WASTED TIME.

HE WAS A PUBLISHER. HE WANTED TO ENTER THE AVANTE~GARDE BOOK TRADE. HE LIKED OUR STUFF, MY WORK-MATE'S WRITING AND MY ILLUSTRATION. "COME UP WITH SOMETHING FOR ME, BOYS," HE PUT IT.

WE LOOKED AT EACH OTHER AND THE WORDS "DARK SPIRAL" SHOT BACK AND FORTH SILENTLY. HE SPOKE THE DOLLAR FIGURES AND WE FELT THE POWER TO ESCAPE.

3.

THAT NIGHT I THOUGHT ABOUT IT. ILLUSTRATED CEREBRAL LITERATURE HE CALLED IT. I DIDN'T KNOW IF HE WANTED TO LAUNDER MONEY OR JUST PLAY PUBLISHER OUT OF BOREDOM, BUT IT WAS MONEY. MONEY FOR THE KIND OF WORK **I** WANTED TO DO.

WE WERE LIKE TWO SCHOOLBOYS WITH THE GIGGLES THE NEXT DAY AT WORK. WE COULDN'T CONCENTRATE AND WALKED AROUND THE BUILDING ALL COCKY.

THE MANAGER PULLED US ASIDE AND TOLD US WE HAD AN ATTITUDE TO TAKE CARE OF. WE RESIGNED, AND KEPT OUR ATTITUDES INTACT.

WE SHOWED THE SNAKE MAN A SCRIPT SYNOPSIS AND SAMPLE STYLE DRAWINGS OF **DARK SPIRAL**. HE LOVED IT. HE WAS GOING TO MAKE US "BIG BIG BIG." WE WERE TO REPORT IN EVERY MONTH FOR A "BULL SESSION."

WE HAD TO FINANCE OUR OWN TIME, BUT I COULD GET BY FOR A WHILE ON MY LAST PAYCHECK. I PRODUCED SOME OF THE BEST WORK IN MY LIFE.

4.

AT THE NEXT BULL SESSION MY WORK-MATE HAD A CONCERN. HE DIDN'T WANT HIS NAME ON **DARK SPIRAL**.

HE FELT UNEASY ABOUT HIS NAME APPEARING IN PUBLIC IN A DRUG STORY. HE THOUGHT THEY MIGHT ARREST HIM.

"NO PROBLEM," THE MAN SAID. HE WOULD PROVIDE HIM AN ALIAS. IT MADE NO DIFFERENCE.

BUT HIS UNEASINESS PUT HIM BEHIND ON HIS WORK. I WAS AHEAD AND HAD NOTHING TO ILLUSTRATE THE NEXT MONTH. I SPENT THE TIME RE~ORGANIZING MY LIFE.

MY MONTH'S NOTICE WAS UP AT THE CORPORATE DORM HOUSE, SO I HAD TO FIND A STUDIO APARTMENT. I TAPPED OUT MY CREDIT CARD TO DO IT, BUT IT WAS WORTH IT. I WOULD LIVE IN A CARDBOARD BOX IF IT MEANT ESCAPING.

THE SOONER WE GOT THIS THING DONE, THE SOONER WE GOT PAID, BUT MY HANDS WERE TIED WITH HIS CONSTANT SCRIPT CHANGES. HE WAS EDITING AND DILUTING ALL THE SUBSTANCE OUT OF HIS OWN WORK.

5.

HE ASKED WHAT HE WOULD DO IF THIS DIDN'T WORK OUT AND HE NEEDED HIS JOB BACK. WHAT IF SOMEONE FROM THE COMPANY RECOGNIZED **ABOUT DARK SPIRAL** AS HIS LIFE.

THEY WOULD SEE THROUGH THE ALIAS. HE WOULD BE BLACKLISTED. I REMINDED HIM OF OUR POWER.

I REMINDED HIM OF US SITTING THERE AT LUNCH TEARING UP THE COMPANY. "I MISS THOSE LUNCHES," HE SAID. I LET IT GO.

I WANTED TO TELL HIM HE'D NEVER HAVE TO GO BACK IF HE JUST TOOK THIS LEAP. BUT I WAS AFRAID WORDS LIKE LEAP WOULD JUST MAKE HIM LOOK DOWN AND FREEZE.

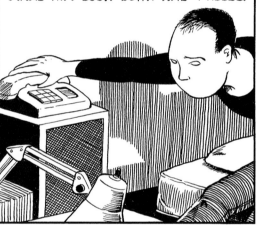

I WENT DOWNTOWN TO CLOSE MY BANK ACCOUNT, SINCE IT WAS DOING NOTHING BUT CHARGING ME A MONTHLY FEE, WHEN I SAW HIM.

I COULD'VE SWORN HE PRETENDED HE DIDN'T SEE ME. I FLAGGED HIM DOWN.

HE DIDN'T SEEM HAPPY TO SEE ME. HE MADE SOME SMALL TALK, THEN ASKED FEARFULLY, "WHAT IF MY MOM FINDS OUT?"

6.

HOW COULD HE FEAR THAT HIS MOTHER, A RELIGIOUS OLD WOMAN WHO LIVED IN THE NEXT TOWN, WOULD EVER HAPPEN ACROSS AN AVANTE-GARDE ART BOOK AND DEDUCE AN ANONYMOUS WRITER WAS HER SON BECAUSE OF REFERENCES TO THINGS ONLY THOSE OF US AT WORK KNEW ABOUT?

"WHEN I SEE THE GUYS FROM WORK THEY JUST SNUB ME," HE ADDED. I HAD NO WAY TO RESPOND TO THAT, AND JUST WALKED AWAY.

I WASN'T SURPRISED TO SEE AN EMPTY CHAIR AT THE NEXT BULL SESSION. I THOUGHT ABOUT BLUFFING HIS ILLNESS, EVEN PIRATING HIS WORK AND CONTINUING THE STORY.

BUT THE SNAKE MAN WAS AHEAD OF ME. MY WORK-MATE PULLED OUT A WEEK AGO, HE TOLD ME. "THAT'S THE BREAKS, KID."

I HEARD THROUGH THE GRAPEVINE THAT HE APOLOGIZED TO THE OLD COMPANY AND GOT HIS COPYWRITER JOB BACK.

I COULDN'T RESIST SKULKING AROUND THE OFFICES AFTER PICKING UP A CHEAP 40-OUNCE BOTTLE OF MALT LIQUOR TO SEE IF IT WAS TRUE.

THERE HE WAS. A LITTLE BOUNCE IN HIS STEP. BACK SAFE, WRITING THE COPY FOR THE STUPID PRODUCTS NOBODY NEEDS. BACK WITH ALL THE BOZOS WHO THOUGHT HIM THEIR ENEMY WHEN HE HAD THE POWER OF FREEDOM.

HIS DARK SPIRAL IS TWICE AS DEEP. THE WRITER WHO HAD JUST ONE STORY, AND HID IT FROM THE REST OF THE WORLD.

7.
End.

81

HAVE YOU EVER WONDERED IF YOU'RE EXPERIENCING THINGS THAT NO ONE ELSE IS? NOT THAT YOU ARE UNIQUE, THAT YOU POSSESS GREATER PERCEPTIVE POWERS, BUT THAT THE WORLD AROUND YOU IS ACTUALLY DIFFERENT THAN THE WORLD SURROUNDING EVERYONE ELSE.

the **GERBIL KING**

HAVE YOU EVER THOUGHT OF DOING WRONG THINGS? BECAUSE MAYBE WHAT YOU'RE SEEING ISN'T REAL?

BECAUSE YOU HAVE TO TEST IT. TO SEE IF THERE'S A REACTION.

SELF-DESTRUCTIVE THINGS. LIFE-THREATENING THINGS.

HAVE YOU EVER WONDERED WHAT WOULD HAPPEN IF YOUR BODY DID THESE THINGS UNCONTROLLABLY,

WHILE YOUR MIND JUST SAT, A HELPLESS SPECTATOR?

1.

AT FIRST THE GERBIL KING SIMPLY ALLOWED ME TO DO THESE WRONG THINGS. 	THEN IT STARTED HELPING ME. 

NOW, IT MAKES ME. 	WHEN I FIRST SAW THE GERBIL KING, I THOUGHT IT WAS A JOKE. SHORTLY AFTER STARTING ON WITH THE COMPANY THREE YEARS AGO... (THAT'S ALL? I FEEL LIKE I SPENT MY LIFE THERE). 

I WAS JUST GETTING USED TO THE GERBILS. FORGETTING MY OLD DREAMS. REALLY FEELING MYSELF HEMMED INTO THOSE LITTLE PLASTIC TUNNELS.

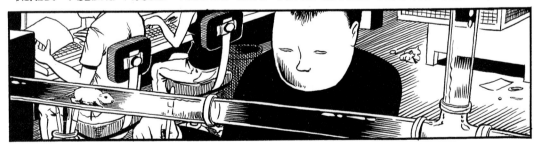

THAT CORPORATE BIOLOGICAL MIND-SCREW DID ITS JOB ON MY MOTIVATION, BUT I DID MANAGE TO RETAIN MY SENSE OF HUMOR. I DIDN'T USE IT TOWARDS ANY OF MY OWN PURSUITS, BUT IT WAS THERE TO FILL THE AIR AND PASS THE TIME AT WORK.

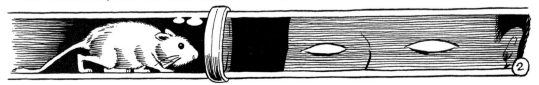

SO WHEN I SAW THIS OVERSIZED GERBIL WITH A CROWN, I ASSUMED SOME OTHER OFFICE PRANKSTER CREATED IT.

WHEN I JOKED AROUND ABOUT THE ABSURDITY OF SOMEONE PUTTING A LITTLE TOY CROWN ON AN OVER-FED GERBIL, MY WORK-MATE CHUCKLED, "YEAH, THAT WOULD BE FUNNY."

BUT SOME ASPECTS OF IT DIDN'T ADD UP. IT WASN'T JUST FAT. IT WAS MUCH TOO LARGE TO BE A GERBIL. ONLY THE HIGHER-UPS IN THE CORPORATION COULD'VE BRED SUCH A THING.

WITH CLOSER EXAMINATION, THE CROWN WASN'T TIED ON. AND IT WASN'T LIBERATED FROM SOME CHEAP CHILDREN'S DOLL OF ROYAL TRAPPINGS, IT WAS A VERY INTRICATE AND BEAUTIFUL THING.

IT WAS SUPERIOR TO THE OTHER RODENTS, LIVING THE FULL THREE YEARS, NOT SEVERAL WEEKS, AND CAME AND WENT FREELY, UNCON-FINED BY THE LABYRINTH OF TUBES... (WENT WHERE? IT WOULD JUST DISAPPEAR!)

I COULDN'T FIGURE ITS PURPOSE AT FIRST. LOOKING BACK, I TRIED TO RECALL WHEN IT WENT FROM A DISTURBING ORNAMENT TO AN ACTIVE PARTICIPANT IN MY LIFE.

I FELT I COULD TRUST MY CLOSEST WORKMATE ON THE SUBJECT, BUT THE DAY I DECIDED TO TALK TO HIM ABOUT IT WAS THE DAY HE WAS CARTED OUT OF THE PRODUCTION ROOM, OPTING TO **BE** A GERBIL RATHER THAN WORK FOR THEM.

84

HIS EYES HAD LESS COGNITION IN THEM THAN THAT ANIMAL, BUT I COULD SWEAR IT STARED AT ME UNTIL SPARKING A MEMORY.

I REMEMBERED THAT I **DID** SPEAK TO MY TRUSTED WORK-MATE ABOUT IT. AND HIS RESPONSE WAS, "THAT **WOULD** BE FUNNY."

NOT "THAT **IS**," BUT "THAT **WOULD**," AS THOUGH HUMORING MY IMAGINATION. HE DIDN'T SEE THE GERBIL KING.

WAS I THE ONLY ONE WHO DID?

I HAD MENTIONED THE CAT LOVER. THAT MARRIAGE AND THOSE MISTAKES WERE MY OWN, AND I CAN'T BLAME THAT PERIOD ON MY MUTE ADVISOR.

I WISH THE HORRIBLE THING **WAS** ACTIVE THEN... I WOULD'VE TAKEN MUCH MORE SATISFYING MEASURES.

I TOLD YOU ABOUT MY BRUSH WITH INTER-OFFICE ROMANCE. THAT'S WHEN I FINALLY COMPREHENDED, WITH RESISTANCE, THAT THE ANIMAL HAD **EXPRESSIONS**. THAT ITS EYES MET MINE. WITH THESE EYES IT MADE SUGGESTIONS.

THE SUGGESTIONS DIDN'T RADICALLY CHANGE MY BEHAVIOR, THOUGH. HOW I INTERACTED WITH THE WOMEN AT WORK WAS BASED ON MY OWN SENSIBILITIES BACK THEN.

4

UNLIKE MY BEHAVIOR DURING THE LAST DAYS BEFORE LEAVING THE COMPANY. LIKE WHEN I MUSED OVER THE SIZE (I'M PARTIAL TO LARGE) OF THE BEHIND OF A TOUGH LITTLE COWGIRL TYPE FROM DOWNSTAIRS.

THE GERBIL KING INSTRUCTED ME TO JUST GO AHEAD AND LIFT UP HER FRILLY SKIRT AND FIND OUT.

I COULD JUST SEE THE POSSIBILITY IN MY MIND. I HAD TO SEE THE RESULT.

SHE TOLD ME IF I COULD JUST, "HOLD MY LITTLE HORSES" UNTIL AFTER WORK I COULD SEE A BIT MORE.

SOMETIMES THE RESULTS WERE A COMPLETE SURPRISE LIKE THAT, OTHER TIMES WOULD GET ME IN SERIOUS TROUBLE. THAT WAS WHAT WAS SO CONFUSING, SO SEDUCTIVE, AND SO DANGEROUS ABOUT THE GERBIL KING. IT SLOWLY EVOLVED FROM A HUMOROUS CIRCUS PERFORMER TO A FRIGHTENING, UNWANTED INVADER OF MY LIFE.

I TOLD YOU ABOUT THE GUN I FOUND, WHICH IS NOW HIDDEN, ALONG WITH **MY** BULLET, IN THE CLOSET. AT THE TIME, I CALLED IT THE ONE REMAINING BULLET, INSTEAD OF THE MORE CORRECT **MY** BULLET, WHICH THE LITTLE KING HAD SINCE CORRECTED ME ON.

IT ALSO FINALLY DAWNED ON ME THAT IT WAS APPEARING **OUTSIDE** OF THE OFFICE. THAT WAS NOT A GOOD SIGN.

WHEN I WOULD PICK UP A SIX-PACK AFTER WORK, THE GERBIL KING WOULD INSIST IT MADE MORE SENSE TO GET A TWELVE-PACK.

BEFORE I COULD REBUKE THAT IT DIDN'T, I COULD SEE MYSELF SAFELY TUCKED IN MY ROOM, IMMENSELY ENJOYING MY SEVENTH THROUGH TWELFTH CANS.

AND THEN I WAS THERE, AND IT SAID, "I TOLD YOU SO."

AND WHEN I WASN'T SATISFIED AT THE CLOSE OF NUMBER TWELVE, IT WOULD TELL ME IT WAS ALRIGHT TO DRIVE TO THE STORE IN THIS STATE AND BUY ONE OF THOSE FORTY-OUNCE MALT LIQUORS THAT THEY TARGET TOWARD THE ETHNIC GROUPS, THE SEMI-HOMELESS, AND FRUSTRATED ARTISTS OF THIS CITY.

6

IT TOLD ME A LITTLE ADRENALINE WAS ALL THAT WAS NEEDED TO PASS THIS SOBRIETY TEST. ADRENALINE, AND THE ABILITY TO SEE IT HAPPEN.

HAVING BEEN GIVEN MY WALKING (DRIVING) PAPERS, IT GLOWED, "I TOLD YOU SO. AND DON'T FORGET THE FORTY-OUNCER."

I TOLD YOU ABOUT THE DOOMED ONE AND MY NERVE-SHATTERING TENURE SPENT NEXT TO HER.

TOWARD THE END I LOST ALL COMPOSURE. WHEN THE GERBIL KING INSTRUCTED ME TO, I JUST SMEARED DOOMED ONE'S FAST-FOOD HAMBURGERS ACROSS HER PASTE-UP ON DEADLINE NIGHT.

NO ONE IN THE OFFICE CHEERED ME FOR THIS, OR CHASTISED ME FOR IT. THEY SEEMED TO KNOW I WAS BEING CONTROLLED BY SOMETHING, YET I NEVER SAW THEM SPEAK TO THE KING DIRECTLY. PERHAPS THEY HAD ALL SPENT THEIR UNPLEASANT TIME WITH IT, AND IT WAS MY TURN FOR THIS RITUAL.

I TOLD YOU ABOUT MY ESCAPES. THE CEMETERIES, THE DRY CREEK BED, THE DISASTROUS DRIVE TO CHILDHOOD HAUNTS. ALL FAILURES.

THEN THE REAL ESCAPE CAME, THE ESCAPE FROM THE COMPANY ITSELF. THE DARK SPIRAL AND THE RESIGNATION. THE GERBIL KING WAS INSTRUMENTAL IN THAT.

⑦

I MENTIONED THAT I MET THE GERBIL KING THREE YEARS AGO. ONLY TWO OF THOSE YEARS WERE SPENT AT THE COMPANY. THE FINAL ONE WAS NOT AS COLORFUL. I STILL BUMPED INTO THE CHARACTERS FROM THE COMPANY ON OCCASION IN THAT CLAUSTROPHOBIC TOWN, BUT MY SOLE COMPANION, REALLY, WAS THE GERBIL KING. THAT YEAR WAS'T LIKE THE OTHER TWO, BUT I'M GOING TO WALK YOU THROUGH THE HIGHLIGHTS. YOU NEED TO KNOW HOW IT ALL BROUGHT ME HERE, TO THESE ABANDONED NUCLEAR MISSILE SILOS ON THE OUTSKIRTS OF TOWN.

OUT OF WORK AND OUT OF LUCK, THIS DIRTY LITTLE ROOMMATE HELPED ORCHESTRATE MY END. WHEN I MOVED OUT OF THE COMPANY'S COMMUNAL HOUSE AND INTO MY TINY STUDIO APARTMENT, IT INSISTED I KEEP THE GUN IN A SAFE PLACE. "THAT LAST BULLET IS **YOUR** BULLET. YOUR END."

IT TAUGHT ME HOW TO LIVE WITHOUT LIVING. THAT THERE WAS NO NEED TO LOOK FOR WORK. THAT ANY JOB WOULD ONLY BE WORSE THAN THE LAST. I HAD TO WORK IN SECRECY ON NEW PUBLISHING PROJECTS, WHICH I SUBMITTED TO THE MAN WHO WAS GOING TO COMMISSION "DARK SPIRAL."

WE MADE A FEW DEALS, BUT IN THE SPAN OF THAT LONG BLEAK YEAR, I ONLY RECEIVED A FEW CHECKS, NOT WORTH THE RELENTLESS DELAYS, REJECTIONS, AND UNANSWERED PHONE CALLS OF FREELANCING.

⑧

THE GERBIL KING TOLD ME TO SELL MY CAR, SINCE I WOULDN'T BE NEEDING TO GO ANYWHERE AGAIN. AFTER THAT, IT WOULD BE TIME TO START SELLING MY RECORD AND COMIC BOOK COLLECTIONS.

I TOLD HIM THAT WOULDN'T BE NECESSARY. I WAS EXPECTING A CHECK IN THE MAIL.

WITH MY ONLY EIGHT DOLLARS, I BOUGHT TWO TWELVE~PACKS OF CHEAP FOUL~TASTING BEER.

BEFORE BEGINNING MY DRINKING RITUAL, I CALLED MY PUBLISHER TO DEMAND ACTION, TO GET MY LIFE ROLLING.

SORRY, BUT EVERYTHING WAS IN LITIGATION WITH THE PARENT CORPORATION, AND IS "ON HOLD" UNTIL FURTHER NOTICE.

"I CAN HELP," THE GERBIL KING ASSURED. "I CAN GET YOU TO THE END SAFELY."

THE NEXT DAY, HAVING FINISHED ONE AND THE BETTER PART OF THE SECOND POOR MAN'S BOX OF BEER, I WAS INTRODUCED TO AN ELABORATE FLOW CHART BY THE GERBIL KING.

"THIS IS HOW IT ALL WORKS," IT STATED. "YOU WILL BE SURPRISED HOW LONG YOU CAN LIVE WITHOUT DOING ANYTHING."

WHAT MY FUZZED VISION BEHELD WAS SOME SORT OF ARCANE BUDGET, WHICH INVOLVED NO REAL TRAD-ITIONAL INCOME. IT WENT THROUGH LIQUIDATION OF ALL MY COLLECTIONS AND POSSESSIONS, BUT TIMED IN SUCH A WAY THAT I WOULDN'T BE WITHOUT THEM UNTIL THE VERY END. THE BULK OF THE INITIAL INCOME WOULD COME FROM CREDIT CARD ADVANCES AND THE STALLING OF BILLS AND RENT. EVENTUALLY, CARD REVOCATION, POWER CUT-OFF, EVICTION, AND SALES OF ALL GOODS WOULD COME TO A SYNCHRONIZED FINALE.

THIS WHOLE ADVENTURE WOULD LAST OVER ONE YEAR.

AND THEN WHAT?

"AND THEN THIS."

AND I ACCEPTED.

10

91

THIS LIFE WITHOUT LIVING WAS... INTERESTING. I LEARNED TO MAKE HOMEMADE BEER AT HALF THE PRICE OF THE CHEAP CANNED STUFF, AND BOUGHT A YEAR'S INGREDIENTS IN BULK.

IT WAS LIKE A CHILDISH ESCAPE FROM REALITY THAT I WOULD HAVE REALLY ENJOYED, EXCEPT FOR THE ANIMAL'S POWER OVER ME.

WHAT IF I CHANGED MY MIND? WHAT IF I GOT TO THIS END AND DECIDED I WANTED TO START OVER? MOVE TO ALASKA AND WORK ON A FISHING BOAT?

WOULD IT LET ME? COULD IT STOP ME? WHAT IF I RAISED A HAND TO IT?

ALTHOUGH I HAD NEVER DARED TOUCH IT, IT HAD CRAWLED UPON ME.

I FELT A SENSATION THAT IF IT CHOSE TO, IT COULD JUST HOOK IT'S PAWS RIGHT DOWN INTO ME. LIKE A FURRY PARASITIC CRAB THAT WOULD CAUSE FURTHER INJURY IF I ATTEMPTED TO REMOVE IT.

I SICKENED OF ITS IMAGE. OF THESE SAME SURROUNDINGS.

AND THEN I FOUND JIMMY. I ADMIT I WAS DRUNK, EMOTIONS HEIGHTENED, BUT THEY WERE GOOD EMOTIONS. THE KIND I HADN'T FELT SINCE AT LEAST COLLEGE.

11

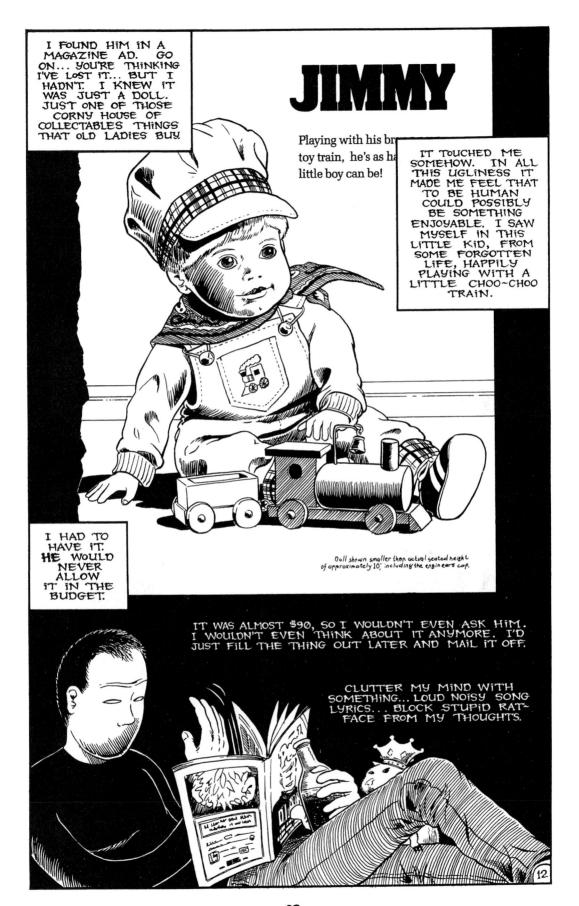

JIMMY

I FOUND HIM IN A MAGAZINE AD. GO ON... YOU'RE THINKING I'VE LOST IT... BUT I HADN'T. I KNEW IT WAS JUST A DOLL. JUST ONE OF THOSE CORNY HOUSE OF COLLECTABLES THINGS THAT OLD LADIES BUY.

Playing with his br[...] toy train, he's as ha[...] little boy can be!

IT TOUCHED ME SOMEHOW. IN ALL THIS UGLINESS IT MADE ME FEEL THAT TO BE HUMAN COULD POSSIBLY BE SOMETHING ENJOYABLE. I SAW MYSELF IN THIS LITTLE KID, FROM SOME FORGOTTEN LIFE, HAPPILY PLAYING WITH A LITTLE CHOO~CHOO TRAIN.

I HAD TO HAVE IT. **HE** WOULD NEVER ALLOW IT IN THE BUDGET.

Doll shown smaller then actual seated height of approximately 10", including the engineers cap.

IT WAS ALMOST $90, SO I WOULDN'T EVEN ASK HIM. I WOULDN'T EVEN THINK ABOUT IT ANYMORE. I'D JUST FILL THE THING OUT LATER AND MAIL IT OFF.

CLUTTER MY MIND WITH SOMETHING... LOUD NOISY SONG LYRICS... BLOCK STUPID RAT~FACE FROM MY THOUGHTS.

12

AND I REALLY DID FORGET ABOUT JIMMY. A FEW MONTHS PASSED. A STRANGE WORLD OF COMPLETE INDULGENCE AND IRRESPONSIBILITY. WHEN THE PACKAGE ARRIVED, I DIDN'T KNOW WHAT TO EXPECT.

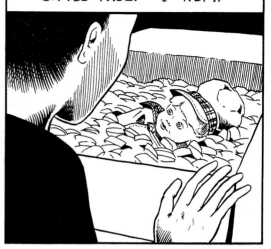

I OPENED IT AND OUT POPPED BRIGHT COLORS AND A HAPPY LITTLE FACE. I WEPT.

I SAT WITH JIMMY FOR HOURS. WHAT A HAPPY LITTLE GUY. HE THINKS THAT TRAIN ONLY HAS SAFE AND PLEASANT DESTINATIONS.

I SET HIM ON MY DRESSER AND DOZED OFF, DREAMING OF JIMMY AND I PILOTING HIS FANTASY FREIGHT TOGETHER.

WE WERE CHUGGING THROUGH BEAUTIFUL PINE MOUNTAINS. DARTING IN AND OUT OF TUNNELS. OVER TRESTLES SPANNING RIVERS AND LONELY ROADS.

94

I HEARD A LOUD RASPING SOUND AND LOOKED ABOUT NERVOUSLY. "S'OKAY." "S'OKAY," JIMMY ASSURED ME.

IT SEEMED TO BE COMING FROM THE LONGEST TRESTLE I'D EVER SEEN, JUST AHEAD.

IT WAS A CRUNCHING SOUND. LIKE A HORDE OF GIANT TERMITES WAS EATING THE BASE OF THE BRIDGE. I LOOKED AT JIMMY WITH A PANIC.

"ALL OKAY!" HE BOASTED, AND GAVE A LOUD, "CHOO CHOO!"

I TRIED TO BELIEVE HIM, BUT AS WE BOARDED THE TRESTLE, I COULD FEEL THE VIBRATIONS. HORRIBLE GNAWING, SCRAPING SOUNDS.

I LOOKED INTO JIMMY'S PROUD, CONFIDENT FACE, TRUSTING HIS ENGINEERING SKILLS.

THEN I FELT THE WORLD CRUMBLE BENEATH US.

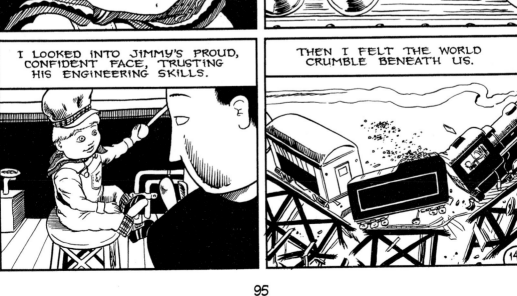

14

95

"JIMMY WRONG! JIMMY WROAUUUUU~NG~NG!"

MY EYES SNAPPED AWAKE AND THE CHEWING AND **SCRAPING** CONTINUED.

IT ATE HIM IT ATE JIMMY THE GODDAMN ANIMAL ATE HIM.

I REACHED OUT TO GRAB HOLD OF IT, AND IT LOCKED INTO ME JUST AS I HAD PRE~CONCEIVED.

ITS CROWN TINKLED TO THE GROUND AS ITS ARMS, NOW MORE LIKE HOOKS, SLID EFFORTLESSLY THROUGH MY FOREARM LIKE FISH HOOKS CURLING INTO LIVE BAIT.

THE ENDS REACHED MY BONE, I THOUGHT, AS I FELT A SICK PRESSURE IN PARTS OF MY BODY I HAD NEVER HAD SENSATIONS BEFORE.

I SHOOK IT AND RAN THROUGH THE DARK STUDIO WITH NOWHERE TO GO, BOUNCING AGAINST WALLS.

15

MY SHIN COLLIDED WITH A SEVEN~GALLON TUB OF HOME BREW, KNOCKING THE TOP OFF, BUT NOT OVERTURNING THE VESSEL.

FOR NO REAL LOGICAL REASON, I SUBMERGED THE INFECTED ARM INTO THE MIXTURE OF HOPS AND YEAST AND WATER.

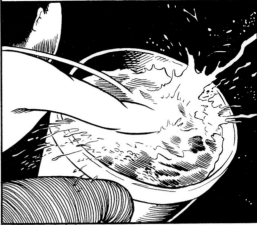

IT IMMEDIATELY FOAMED UP INTO A FOUL GREY HEAD. A STENCH LIKE WET DOGS AND DEAD BIRDS BLEW OUT, FOLLOWED BY A BUBBLING, SYRUPY RED~BROWN GEL.

OVERCOME WITH THE SENSATION OF LOSING MY RIGHT ARM, I PASSED OUT IN THE DARK, TINY ROOM THAT WOULD BE MY LAST SOLITARY PLACE OF RESIDENCE.

I WOKE UP IN A HOSPITAL WITH A FUNCTIONING RIGHT ARM DOTTED WITH FOUR PERFECTLY~HEALED SCARS, LEADING ME TO IMAGINE I WAS IN A COMA FOR WEEKS.

THEY TOLD ME IT WAS JUST LAST NIGHT THAT THE POLICE BROUGHT ME IN. MY LANDLORD CALLED THE POLICE OVER THE NOISE, AND, GIVEN MY DELINQUENCY ON THE RENT, TOOK ADVANTAGE OF MY SITUATION AND HAD THE LOCKS CHANGED.

16

REALIZING THAT THE HOLES IN MY ARM WERE SOME SORT OF HALLUCINATION, I ASKED WHY I WAS TAKEN HERE.
"ASIDE FROM THE FACT THAT YOU WERE HALF-DROWNED IN A LARGE TUB OF BEER," THE DOCTOR PUFFED, "ONE LIGHT CONCUSSION TO THE HEAD AND A SMALL LACERATION TO THE SHIN."

THEY GAVE ME WHAT THEY CALLED MY EFFECTS, (MAKING ME FEEL LIKE I BELONGED IN THE MORGUE) WHICH THE POLICE HAD ROUNDED UP BEFORE THE LAND~ LORD STARTED GRABBING MY CDs.

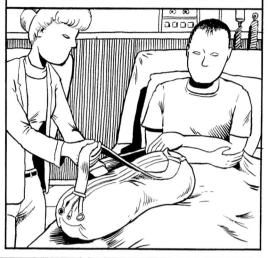

I GUESS THEY FELT I WAS ENTITLED TO SOME CLOTHES AND MY WALLET AND—

YAAAGGH!

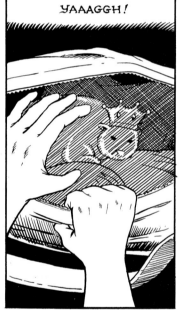

"YOU WERE HOLDING THAT QUITE DETERMIN~ ATELY, FROM WHAT I'M TOLD," THE NURSE OFFERED.

IT'S STUFFED. WHAT THE HELL?

MY FLOW CHART TO SUICIDE WAS CUT SHORT, IT SEEMED. A STUFFED TOY BROUGHT ME TO THE STATUS OF STREET PERSON.

IN MY CONFUSION AT THE BUS DEPOT, I GOT ON THE OUTGOING BY MISTAKE, MEANING TO HEAD BACK TO TOWN AND BREAK INTO MY APARTMENT IF NECESSARY TO GET MY STUFF.

17

I EXIT ON THE LAST STOP AT THE EDGE OF TOWN BEFORE THE BUS MAKES ITS RETURN TRIP. I DIDN'T THINK IT WOULD COME TO THIS. I THOUGHT IT WAS JUST A GAME.

AN OLD MAN, HIS WALK MUCH TOO CHIPPER, CAME WALKING STRAIGHT TOWARDS ME.

"GOIN' TO THE SILOS?" HE ASKED. "HOPE YOU BROUGHT YOUR FLASHLIGHT!"

I JUST SHOOK MY HEAD WITH MISCOMPREHENSION.

HE THOUGHT FOR SURE I WAS GOING TO THE NUCLEAR MISSILE SILOS, SEEING I WAS CARRYING A PACK AND POINTED TOWARDS THE TRAIL.

"PEOPLE EXPLORE 'EM ALL THE TIME. KENNEDY BUILT 'EM BACK IN '61."

"OBSOLETE BEFORE THEY WERE EVEN PUT ON LINE. THAT'S YER DAD'S TAX MONEY, SO GO CHECK 'EM OUT."

I COULDN'T BELIEVE IT. IT WAS FITTING THOUGH. ONE LAST APOCALYPTIC SIGHT-SEEING.

WE JUST CAN'T LIVE WITH EACH OTHER, CAN WE?

19

I THOUGHT AT LEAST ONE OF THOSE OFFICE WOMEN COULD BE A COMPANION. COULD ERASE MY SAD MEMORY OF THE ONE WHO LOVED CATS MORE THAN PEOPLE.

I THOUGHT MY ACID-DROPPING WORK-MATE WAS A COMEDIC VISIONARY, AND WE COULD CREATE TOGETHER.

BUT NONE OF US CAN TOLERATE EACH OTHER. IT'S A CRUEL JOKE.

TO HAVE NOTIONS OF WHAT IT SHOULD BE, AND THOSE NOTIONS BE UNOBTAINABLE.

TO HAVE DESIRES THAT CAN'T BE—

20

101

I LOOKED AROUND FOR THE GERBIL KING'S REACTION TO IT ALL.

WHERE I THOUGHT I SAW HIM CROUCHED, JUST TURNED OUT TO BE A RUSTY TIN CAN IN A PATCH OF DEAD GREY WEEDS.

WAS HE JUST A MANIFESTATION OF SUICIDE IN MY OWN MIND? I DON'T KNOW.

WHAT DISTURBS ME, DESPITE THE FORTUNE I FEEL, IS TRYING TO ACCEPT ALL THE VARIABLES THAT GOT ME HERE.

WITH THE ABSENCE OF ONE... THE WRONG BUS, THE OLD MAN... THIS WOULDN'T BE.

IS OUR DESPAIR OR HAPPINESS THAT DELICATE? OR DID I ENDURE ALL THE PAIN BY DESIGN TO REACH THIS POINT?

I STOP MY INQUISITIVE THOUGHTS, AND SIMPLY ENJOY.

23
End.

EPILOGUE 1: BEYOND THE HABITRAILS

THE MISSILE SILO GIRL ROMANCE WAS FAST AND POWERFUL. SHE WAS AN ARTIST
AND AN ENTREPRENEUR, RENTING A MODEST DOWNTOWN ROOM. WHAT COULD HAVE
BEEN BETTER FOR THIS YOUNG MAN? IN DAYS I HAD MOVED IN. IN WEEKS WE
HAD WED. SHE HAD YOUNG CHILDREN FROM A FORMER MARRIAGE, BUT
DEFIED THE MAINSTREAM PLAN BY ALLOWING CUSTODY TO THEIR
FATHER IN ANOTHER TOWN. THEY WERE OUT OF SIGHT, OUT OF MIND.

COUNT OFF FOUR YEARS, AND THE PICTURE MORPHED. THE CHILDREN RETURNED
TO THE MOTHER'S DEN, THE POVERTY OF BOHEMIA BECAME UNACCEPTABLE,
AND THE SUBURBAN HOUSE, SAFE AND NEAR SCHOOLS, REQUIRED. LIFE
TRANSFORMED AROUND ME INTO SOMETHING UNRECOGNIZABLE. MY SAMENESS
IN THE WAKE OF CHANGE BECAME A LIABILITY. I WAS SERVING AS AN
IMPOSTER IN A WORLD I HAD SHUNNED ALL MY LIFE. IT WAS TIME TO MOVE ON.

YOU RECALL MY JOURNEY THROUGH THE DRY CREEK BED, AND THE ANONYMOUS, ALIEN TOWN? I DECIDED TO MOVE THERE, AND BECOME THE ANONYMOUS, ALIEN MAN.

I COULD CUT MYSELF OFF FROM THAT OLD LIFE. I WOULD NEVER BUMP INTO THEM AGAIN. THE NEWSPAPER STAFF, OLD FRIENDS, EVEN FAMILY. THIS WAS MY PLAN. TO UN-KNOW EVERYONE.

DURING MY YEARS OF POVERTY, I DID ACHIEVE MY GOAL OF MAKING COMICS. A GREAT MANY COMICS. SOME SIMPLE PHOTOCOPIES, SOME LAVISHLY PRODUCED. THEY MADE ME A TENUOUS LIVING AT BEST. I DECIDED TO MAKE MORE.

WHY WOULD I DO THIS AGAIN, YOU MAY ASK? DIDN'T I RECALL THE DARK SPIRAL FAILURE, THE ALCOHOL-SOAKED PERIOD OF MAKING MORE BEER THAN COMICS, THE EMBARRASSING YEARS MARRIED TO THE BREADWINNER. COULDN'T I JUST GO OUT AND GET A JOB AND DO THIS FOR FUN?

NO. THIS WAS WHAT I WAS WIRED TO DO. I COULDN'T JUST TURN IT OFF. I WAS COMMITTED TO KEEP MAKING THEM. NEWER, BETTER, **MORE!** MY FIRE COULD NOT BE SNUFFED.

THINGS WERE DIFFERENT THIS TIME. I HAD A NEW, SOUNDER FINANCIAL PLAN. THE GERBIL KING WAS GONE. REALLY, TRULY GONE, AND GONE WITH HIM WAS THE SUICIDE PACT. THAT WAS A DARK RECLUSION. THIS WAS A BRIGHT-WHITE RECLUSION. I HAVE UN-KNOWN EVERYONE. NO DISTRACTIONS.

MY TINY APARTMENT BECAME A FACTORY. FORGING COMICS PAGES FROM MY FIRE LIKE A BLACKSMITH.

I KEPT THE JARHEAD IN CHECK.
I TOOK LONG, HEALTHY CYCLE RIDES,
TWENTY MILES EVERY OTHER DAY.
I WAS KICKING ASS.

BUT EVENTUALLY, THE BAD THINGS
STARTED UP AGAIN. I CAME HOME,
AND MY DOOR WAS AJAR.
HAD I BEEN ROBBED?

INSTEAD, THERE WAS A DOG INSIDE.
A BIG, WHITE DOG. IT WAS EATING
SOMETHING. WHAT COULD IT
POSSIBLY WANT IN HERE?

IN HORROR I SAW IT HAD EATEN
SEVERAL OF MY ORIGINAL COMICS
PAGES. THIS MADE NO SENSE.

I SHOOED IT OUT FRANTICALLY.
IT SEEMED UNCONCERNED WITH ME,
EXCEPT FOR THE ODD FACT THAT IT SMILED.

THE MONTHS
ROLLED BY.

THE
INTERNET
WAS BORN.

IT MADE A GREAT
WAY FOR ME TO ORDER
THINGS ONLINE AND
HAVE EVEN LESS
INTERACTION WITH THE
PEOPLE OF THIS CITY.

107

THERE WAS INTERNET DATING. THIS WAS THE EXCEPTION TO THE ISOLATION. I WENT ON COUNTLESS OF THESE DATES. NONE RESULTED IN FRIEND OR LOVER.

I LIKED TO RISE EARLY AND DRAW WITH COFFEE. THIS WAS MY FAVORITE TIME OF DAY. SO PEACEFUL. SO MINE. BUT SOMETHING WASN'T RIGHT...

AGAIN, THE DOG! I HAD BEEN AROUND THE WHOLE APARTMENT THAT MORNING. IT WAS EMPTY, AND LOCKED! THIS WAS NOT POSSIBLE. THE DOG HAD DEVOURED DOZENS OF PAGES.

IT ALWAYS SNIFFED OUT THE UN-PUBLISHED PAGES, TOO. UNABLE TO FIGURE OUT HOW IT WAS GETTING IN, I RESOLVED TO MAKE PHOTOCOPIES OF EVERY PAGE I DREW EVERY DAY SO THIS WOULD NEVER HAPPEN AGAIN.

AT NIGHT I WOULD TEND TO MY FINANCIAL MASTER PLAN. MY ELABORATE CHARTS AND SPREADSHEETS. MY VARIOUS ACCOUNTS. ALL WAS WELL.

WALKING DOWNTOWN I RAN INTO SOMEONE FROM THE OLD NEWSPAPER.

I WAS NERVOUS ABOUT HEARING ALL THE OLD DRAMA, BUT HE HAD MOVED ON.

HE HAD NOT ONLY LEFT THE NEWSPAPER, HE LEFT THE GRAPHIC DESIGN WORLD BEHIND ENTIRELY.

HE WORKED FOR A GIANT ELECTRICITY UTILITY. HE SAID IT WAS HONEST WORK, AND IF I EVER WANTED AN "IN" JUST LET HIM KNOW.

STERN ELECTRIC

GOOD FOR HIM. AND THANKS, BUT NO THANKS.

AND AGAIN, THE SMILING DOG GETS IN. IT EATS THE PAGES AND THE PHOTOCOPIES.

HOW CAN THIS BE HAPPENING? I KEEP DOING THIS WORK BETTER AND BETTER, BUT IT DISAPPEARS FASTER AND FASTER. HOPELESSLY, I JUST STICK WITH THE PROGRAM.

STICK WITH IT, THAT IS, UNTIL MY BLACK TUESDAY. I AM SERVED NOTICE TO APPEAR IN COURT.

IT SEEMS MY FINANCIAL PLAN WAS INGENIOUS, BUT NOT SO SOUND. I SIMPLY PAID ALL MY LIVING EXPENSES WITH CREDIT. A MYSTERIOUS BENE-FACTOR WHO REFERRED TO HERSELF AS "FAN X" PAID THE PRINTING BILLS. THEN I RECEIVED THE PROCEEDS FROM THE COMICS (WHICH WAS ALWAYS LESS THAN THE LIVING EXPENSES).

EVEN WITH A BENEFACTOR, IT WAS ALL GOING IN THE NEGATIVE.

SHE LIVED IN A HOSPITAL, AND SAID ALL SHE WANTED WAS TO SEE MY COMICS BE REALIZED, NO STRINGS ATTACHED. I DIDN'T KNOW IF SHE WAS A NERDY RECLUSE, A TRAGIC BEAUTY, OR IN FACT A MAN. I JUST TOOK THE OFFER AND RAN TO THE ALIEN CITY TWO YEARS PRIOR.

SHE SUDDENLY STOPPED PAYING OR COMMUNICATING, AND THE DEBT HIT THE WALL.

DIFFERENT PLAN, SAME END RESULT. DIFFERENT FALSE INCOME, SAME FAILURE. THE WHITE FIRE OF COMICS BLINDED ME TO THESE REALITIES, SO OBVIOUS TO ALL THE OTHERS WHO DROPPED OUT OF THIS DYING ART FORM YEARS AGO.

I AM THIRTY-FIVE YEARS OLD, WITH NO HOPE OF MAKING A LIVING WITH THIS THING I LOVE. THIS SUDDEN SHIFT, AND THE SMILING DOG EATING MY WORK, PLUNGED ME INTO A SILENT, STATIC SHOCK.

NOT LIKE THE ACTIVE, PRONOUNCED MELANCHOLY THAT MADE ME ROLL UP MY SLEEVES AND DEVISE INSANE PLANS. THIS WAS COMPLETELY PASSIVE. A LACK OF ANY INTEREST IN ANYTHING.

THE BIKE RIDES, THE INTERNET DATING, EATING, DRINKING... NOW ALL GREY AND SEEN THROUGH A TUNNEL VISION. IT WAS AS THOUGH I HAD BEEN ON SPEED THE LAST TWENTY YEARS WHILE MAKING COMICS AND NOW I WANTED A DEEP COMA SLEEP.

I DID THE UNTHINKABLE. I CALLED THE OLD CO-WORKER AND GOT AN INTERVIEW WITH THE BIG STATE UTILITY. THIS WAS SURVIVAL. EMOTIONLESS SURVIVAL.

AND SO STARTED MY NEW CAREER. HE WAS RIGHT. THIS WAS HONEST WORK. I WOULD TAKE IT A DAY AT A TIME... GET OUT OF DEBT... GET RECHARGED. IT'S NOT SO BAD.

IT IS TWENTY-FIVE YEARS LATER, THE YEAR 2022, AND IT IS MY RETIREMENT. I HAD MANY REASONS TO LEAVE THIS COMPANY, AND MANY TO STAY. IT ALL EVENED OUT.

POVERTY AND DEBT ARE A FUZZY MEMORY, AND THE CARROTS THAT KEPT ME HERE ALL THESE YEARS MAKE ME SAFE AND COMFORTABLE.

I DON'T KNOW IF ANYONE PLANS A PARTY. I WON'T FIND OUT, AS I TOLD EVERYONE TOMORROW IS MY LAST DAY. BUT I TOLD HUMAN RESOURCES THAT TODAY IS MY LAST DAY. GOOD~BYE.

I'VE HEARD ABOUT A TOWN, FAR OFF IN THE DESERT, WHERE OLD COMICS ARTISTS GO.

EPILOGUE 2: GHOST TOWN STUDIO

MAYBE I WOULD MEET SOME OTHER OLD ARTISTS. IT WOULD BE FUN TO REMINISCE AFTER A QUARTER-CENTURY~LONG SILENCE. I HAVE ARRIVED AT MY NEW HOME WITH MY MEAGER BELONGINGS. THE MINIMUM FOR SURVIVAL, NEARLY LIKE A CAMPOUT.

I SEE,
    IN TRUTH,
        IT IS A GHOST TOWN.

THIS DOESN'T BOTHER ME. I TAKE LONG WALKS AND EXPLORE. I DRIVE DEEP INTO CANYONS. I HIKE RIDGES AND PEAKS. I REALLY LOVE THIS PLACE.

I FIND THE RUINS OF THE GIANT COMICS PUBLISHERS THAT RULED IN THE LAST CENTURY.

AS WELL AS THE ONES FROM JUST A FEW DECADES AGO.

NATIONWIDE COMI

DARK BISON COMICS

IMAGINARY COMICS

JUST WHAT DID I ACHIEVE WITH THIS LIFE OF LABOR, AND WHERE HAS IT ALL GONE? MORE POINTEDLY, YOU MAY WONDER, IS HOW DO I LIVE OUT HERE ALL ALONE IN A GHOST TOWN?

LET ME TELL YOU ABOUT BOTH OF THOSE THINGS.

I MADE COMICS ABOUT A GIANT ALIEN HERO OF JAPAN. SO MANY THAT THEY FILL TWO PHONE BOOK-LIKE REPRINT VOLUMES.

ULTRA KLUTZ

ONCE EVERY TWO WEEKS, I DRIVE INTO TOWN, WHERE I TAKE A SMALL STACK OF BILLS FROM A MAGIC MACHINE.

ATM

I MADE TONS OF ESOTERIC SMALL PRESS FILLER, MOST OF IT CRAP, BUT IT STILL AMUSES ME LIKE AN OLD DIARY.

THIS STACK OF BILLS IS NOTHING COMPARED TO THE AMOUNTS MY UTILITY PEERS WILL NEED TO MAINTAIN THEIR EXPENSIVE LIVES OF COMFORT. AND SO IT WILL LAST VIRTUALLY FOREVER OUT HERE. I BUY FOOD, WATER, GAS, AND SOME WHISKEY AND CIGARS AS MY LUXURIES.

I MADE SILLY COMICS ABOUT A BATTLING FATHER AND SON. IT WASN'T SO WELL REGARDED, BUT I DIDN'T CARE. I LIKE IT.

www.FATHERANDSONTOON.COM

I HAVE A DUSTY OLD WILD BURRO FOR COMPANIONSHIP.

I MADE COMICS ABOUT A SURREAL ALTERNATE UNIVERSE OF HISTORICAL FICTION. IT WAS VERY WELL REGARDED BUT NOT BY ENOUGH PEOPLE TO SEE TO THE ENDING. IT DOES NOT END. THAT IS A BIT SAD, I ADMIT.

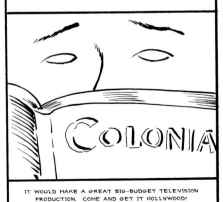

IT WOULD MAKE A GREAT BIG-BUDGET TELEVISION PRODUCTION. COME AND GET IT HOLLYWOOD!

A FLOCK OF PIGEONS ROOSTS IN ONE OF THE SHACKS. THEY LET ME VISIT WITH THEM AND GIVE ME NO END OF ENTERTAINMENT.

SOME FOR ME?
SOME FOR ME?
SOME FOR ME?

I DREW THIS STORY YOU NOW READ. SOME CHAPTERS WERE PUBLISHED SEVERAL TIMES... ONE WAS NOMINATED FOR AN AWARD... I EVEN BROKE MY SILENCE AND DREW MORE OF IT WHILE OUT HERE IN THE DESERT.

THAT'S IT. THAT'S ALL. LIFE IS JUST THIS SIMPLE NOW.

I COULD HAVE WORKED MY WHOLE LIFE AT SOMETHING SAFE LIKE THAT UTILITY, BUT THEN I WOULD JUST HAVE TWICE AS MUCH SURPLUS MAGIC MONEY, YET NO ACHIEVEMENTS TO LOOK BACK ON.

ON THE OTHER HAND, IF I CONTINUED TO LABOR OVER THE COMICS ALL THOSE YEARS, WELL, I WOULD HAVE NO MONEY AND WOULD NOW BE CONTINUING TO STRUGGLE IN OLD AGE.

IT ALL WORKED OUT. ESCAPE #4: GHOST TOWN STUDIO.

AND THE VIEWS ARE AMAZING...

END.

AFTERWORD

This edition has a lot to do with time and reflection and things coming full circle. When I first drew the early chapters of this novella in 1989, I would press them into everyone's faces (friends, family, co-workers), saying proudly LOOK WHAT I HAVE DONE (including some of the staff of the newspaper where it all began, if you can imagine). I seemed to have had no filter in those early years, but let's follow the circle (the Dark Spiral?). In the 1996 second edition of *Habitrails*, Steve Bissette said so kindly and earnestly, "Jeff knows, in his heart of hearts, *Through the Habitrails* is worth keeping in print. Forever." I was flattered but shrugged it all off as the whole comics business was shrugging me off one too many times that year. I quit comics "forever" (for the first time) shortly after. From 1998 onward I would never tell a co-worker soul about *Habitrails*. The filter became an iron curtain.

Unlike the autobiographical aspect of the epilogue, I didn't quite go from comics to nothingness for 25 years, but went on to make many comics part time while holding a day job until the next "quit comics forever" in 2004. At which time pops up this review by Matt Fraction (reprinted in this introduction) saying, "I can't imagine Nicholson being particularly enthused about HABITRAILS anymore. . ." and he was right. At that time *Habitrails* was buried under a rock. I would not hand a copy of that book to anyone in my personal life.

Now ahead ten more years to 2014, and Drew Ford approaches me and wants to do this edition. My first instinct is that here is yet another crackpot offer that comes to nothing. But we talk and he talks me into it. When I read the old chapters that I haven't read for many, many years they impressed me. Don't take that as egotistical. I was embarrassed by them for a time as too much the bitter young man, and as I said, I didn't share them anymore. But I felt as though I were an outside observer looking in on them, that they were tight and concise (at least the first half was). With nudging from Dover, I decided to kick Cat Lover's presence mostly out of the novella. That chapter wasn't originally intended as a part of *Through the Habitrails*; anyway (those of you who have the early editions, notice the lack of Chad Woody's distinctive lettering). It was sort of a spin-off project that I ended up selling to TABOO because I needed the page rate to pay the rent. In my current option, it is too off-topic, overly long, and distracting from the core themes of *Through the Habitrails*. This gave me the chance to heavily revise and trim the final Gerbil King chapter, also too long and having too much Cat Lover in it. Now that character is just alluded to in a few of the chapters, and I hope you agree the whole novella is more focused.

And then Drew asks me: do I want to draw more? No way, I haven't drawn any new comics since 2004. I am done. Then I dust off a synopsis of a sequel I wrote back in 1996 regarding, amongst other things, a benign dog who eats away my career. And I dust off a scribbly notion about a Ghost Town Studio that I told my Facebook friends in 2011 or so that I would make a comic out of and immediately procrastinated it into noth- ingness. So yeah, I'm going to do some new pages. I'm going to take my old drawing table that my parents bought me for my thirteenth birthday and has born every 1,000+ comics pages I have ever drawn and has been in the garage for five years as a place to sit all my backpacking gear on top of and pull it back in the house and draw some fucking comics. Gasp. Wheeze.

Then I see, yes, Matt was right—I wasn't "particularly enthused" in 2004, and yes, Steve was right—I totally did care in my "heart of hearts" in 1996, and it's all spiraling back down to now in this new edition and I do care again. It's like the NO END chapter with the young man chal- lenging what the old man will want and the old man defying what the young man would want him to want and I drew 10 new pages and Steve did a new intro and I wrote a new Afterword and we are spinning into the Dark Spiral again and. . . Gee, thanks, Drew, look what you've done.

When this began in 1989 I looked at the present and peered into the future and it was the Dark Spiral. Now I look at the present and it is still somewhat a spiral, but not so dark really. I peer into the future and it is okay. Maybe even good. As good as the retired Habitrails man has it out there in the desert. We'll see.

Jeff Nicholson
9/11/2015

AVON FREE PUBLIC LIBRARY

3 2529 13833 3513

7/16

ABOUT THE AUTHOR

Jeff Nicholson is a native of the San Francisco Bay area. Born in 1962, Jeff has made residence in eleven different cities around Northern California in his lifetime, earned his BA in Graphic Design from CSU, Chico, and has enjoyed a career in Geographic Information Systems (GIS) since 1998.

Influenced by an odd mix of *Mad* magazine, Jack Kirby, and underground comics, Jeff drew numerous homemade color comics in the 1970s in his early teens. Enrolling in college at age sixteen, he started work on his first official underground comic, *Ultra Klutz* (a torturous parody of Ultraman), which was self-published in 1981. Rebooted as a zine in 1984, and again in 1986 as a direct sales comic, *Ultra Klutz* sold 18,000 copies at the height of the "black and white boom" and went on for 31 issues plus a sequel.

All told, Jeff Nicholson created over 1,500 pages of comics in his 25-year career, both self-published (*Ultra Klutz, Lost Laughter, Colonia*) and published by major publishers (*Father & Son*–Kitchen Sink Press, *The Dreaming*–Vertigo/DC), and the work you hold now, which over time has been a hybrid of self-publishing and in conjunction with Spiderbaby Grafix and Tundra Publishing. Jeff received a total of six Will Eisner Comics Industry Award nominations from 1993–1999 during the peak years of his diverse output.

Jeff "retired" from comics in 2005, and aside from a few animation projects, has enjoyed his free time backpacking in the High Sierras and driving around the deserts of the Great Basin with his wife, Roxanne.

AVON FREE PUBLIC LIBRARY
281 COUNTRY CLUB ROAD, AVON CT 06001

www.fatherandsontoon.com